one
space
living

one
space
living

CYNTHIA INIONS   photography by ANDREW WOOD

RYLAND
PETERS
& SMALL

Designer   Megan Smith

Senior editor   Annabel Morgan

Location researchers   Nadine Bazar and Kate Brunt

Production   Patricia Harrington

Publishing director   Anne Ryland

Head of design   Gabriella Le Grazie

Stylist   Cynthia Inions

Plans   Russell Bell

First published in the United Kingdom in 1999
by Ryland Peters & Small
Cavendish House, 51–55 Mortimer Street,
London W1N 7TD
10 9 8 7 6 5 4 3 2 1

Text © Cynthia Inions 1999
Design and photographs © Ryland Peters & Small 1999

Produced by Sun Fung Offset Binding Co., Ltd
Printed and bound in China

ISBN 1 900518 98 8

A CIP record for this book is available from
the British Library

Front jacket: Alistair Hendy and John Clinch's apartment
in London, designed by Alistair Hendy. Back jacket: Jeff
Priess and Rebecca Quaytman's apartment in New York,
designed by Fernlund and Logan Architects.

contents

introduction

For more and more people, a single-space home is a solution to the challenge of contemporary living. One-space living offers the freedom to organize your home to suit the new informality in the way we live and spend time with family and friends, the diversity of modern lifestyles and the demand for a multi-functional environment.

Designing and planning a single-space living environment from scratch or simply revising a conventional interior presents the opportunity to use your space more efficiently and imaginatively, to create a welcoming and flexible home environment and enjoy a new sense of light, openness and integration. Introducing permanent partitions or reconfiguring space with flexible dividers can provide a comfortable and essential degree of separation between public and private areas without compromising the unity or versatility of the overall space.

The one-space home utilizes a new and dynamic vocabulary of space, light and freedom of choice. This book presents an inspiring and individual collection of many different one-space environments, from radical conversions of industrial buildings to simple low-level reworkings of typical domestic spaces, from concrete and glass constructions to family-friendly environments with plenty of colour and comfort.

opposite A dynamic conversion of a post-office sorting depot provides a versatile split-level interior.

above left A low mobile table made out of concrete slabs adds an industrial element to a relaxing zone.

above centre Flip-up and pull-down panels expose and enclose different elements of this kitchen area as desired.

above right Removing part of the floor in a two-level loft radically improves light distribution and openness.

living in

a single space

why one space? | options | help

why one space?

ONE-SPACE LIVING OFFERS A NEW FREEDOM OF CHOICE IN WHERE AND HOW TO LIVE. THERE ARE ALL KINDS OF OPPORTUNITIES TO CONVERT OR DEVELOP POTENTIAL ONE-SPACE ENVIRONMENTS, AND EVERY PROJECT PRESENTS A CHALLENGING AND DIFFERENT PACKAGE OF DIVERSE AND CREATIVE POSSIBILITIES.

Freedom | In a one-space environment, everything is up for review. Conventional preconceptions about designing and planning a domestic interior are completely irrelevant – in a one-space home, there is no need to separate and confine everyday activities within a restrictive traditional layout. Whether you take on an existing open-plan scheme and adapt it, reconfigure a conventional space, or convert a previously non-domestic unit, the design and planning decisions will always be specific to every project.

Of all the possibilities, converting or refitting a non-domestic environment offers the maximum creative freedom. It allows you to develop an original space, removed from any references to domestic architectural proportions, structures and materials. Alternatively, stripping a domestic interior to an empty shell and beginning again, if possible and cost-efficient, can be an equally exciting undertaking, and is well worth it if the building is of special architectural interest or in an area where you specifically want to live. Nevertheless, be aware that, apart from demanding a large budget, projects like these are huge undertakings and require a great deal of commitment, time, energy and effort.

Less ambitious schemes offer varying degrees of creative freedom. Sometimes an existing open-plan arrangement is a good starting point for modification and improvement. Bringing a new sense of harmony and integration to a space by introducing uniform floor coverings or lighting systems, for example, can create the impression of single-space living without requiring massive disruption or expense. Introducing change, on any scale, is vital to individualize space.

left The raw architecture of a former printworks provided an inspiring starting point for this new domestic scheme. Visible metal support beams, concrete paving-slab flooring and heavy-duty professional catering equipment are all in keeping with the industrial aesthetic of the space.

Sense of space | A sense of space is life-enhancing, and makes all the difference between a dynamic, welcoming environment and an unappealing one. Single-space living offers you an opportunity to make the most of the available space, whatever its size or shape.

There are many different ways to create or increase a sense of space, from large-impact structural alterations to a simple process of paring down and elimination. Radical transformations, like removing walls or floors to create a double-height space, increasing the size of windows or converting redundant roof space, will all increase a feeling of openness and improve light distribution. However, maximum openness is not always the best way forward. Contrasts between openness and enclosure can provide an important dimension to experiencing a space, so contracting part of a space instead of expanding it is an alternative option.

In conventional interiors, it is not always possible to remove internal walls, either for structural reasons or because imposing a radical open-plan layout will spoil the overall proportions of the space. If this is the case, reducing the size of walls, either vertically or horizontally, adding portholes or creating internal windows will all provide a degree of openness and sense of connection while preserving original divisions and supports.

It is possible to increase the perception of space with reorganization on a small scale. Eliminating excess furniture and clutter is an effective and immediate way to increase space. For example, only allow sufficient chairs around a table, and remove and store any surplus. Keep kitchen surfaces clear of gadgets and stack magazines and books in storage systems. Everything, no matter how appealing or valuable, takes up space, so subtract anything redundant or excessive and see the difference.

this page and opposite left In a loft conversion, removing part of an upper floor and adding a double-height window optimizes light and space.

opposite centre An upper gallery provides a series of areas for relaxing, sleeping, bathing and working. Sliding panels make flexible dividers.

opposite right The sleek, minimalist kitchen area is kept deliberately free of clutter, adding to the overall sense of space and light.

Flexibility |

One-space living offers the potential for maximum flexibility, allowing you to optimize space. The traditional Japanese interior demonstrates how to manipulate space to suit different activities by using panels or screens to sub-divide a single unit into different configurations. The principle of finding ways to divide a space and provide degrees of separation and privacy without compromising a sense of unity is a good model for contemporary environments.

Paper blinds, freestanding screens and fabric dividers all work effectively as low-cost, temporary fittings. For example, a bath in an unusual position in full view of a sitting area gains privacy with a length of fabric, while an apartment can sub-divide into separate living and work areas with ceiling-to-floor lengths of paper hanging from hooks. Architectural devices such as transparent or solid panels, rotating sections of wall and vast doors that fold out, slide across or swing into place as partitions are also ingenious solutions, although such divisions are more permanent. For true flexibility, provide several options for both openness and enclosure, thus meeting your changing needs without compromising flexibility by committing to a permanent configuration of space.

| FLEXIBILITY IS AN ESSENTIAL ELEMENT OF ONE-SPACE LIVING |

Integration | One-space living allows you to create a multi-functional living environment that will meet all your needs. By grouping activities into zones, you can create an efficient and enjoyable place in which to live. Yet as different activities tend to overlap, working out how best to combine activities in zones and how to integrate zones within a single space is a complex issue.

Before making any decisions about integration, first consider the multitude of everyday activities that take place in your home. Group any related activities together in one zone or in zones that are in close proximity to each other. Position zones according to frequency of use, ease of access and proximity to other zones. Consider the progression from public to private zones and install flexible dividers or incorporate an intermediate cross-over area between the two.

The main challenge of integration is maintaining an intrinsic quality of openness while making adequate provision for privacy and reclusion. Striking this balance is a key factor in determining how comfortable it is to

live in a one-space home, especially if you are part of a busy family unit with people of all ages sharing the same space. Be aware of the day-to-day demands on your space and use dividers to screen more intimate zones, such as bathing or sleeping areas.

Often, the ideal solution is a reconciliation of what is practical, logical and cost-efficient. Special architectural or structural features can pre-designate an area for specific use or suggest a sequence of zones. The position of utilities and drains, for example, will indicate possible locations for kitchen sinks and baths. Even so, with resourceful planning and possible re-routing of service systems, it is possible to avoid over-compartmentalizing activities in a conventional way. After all, freedom, flexibility and individual expression are the whole point of one-space living.

opposite left Widening existing openings, removing doors and reducing the height of internal walls are all low-key ways of improving integration between formerly separate areas in conventional domestic interiors.

opposite right A former work-shop in Paris provides a quirky open-plan interior. Lowering the kitchen floor made enough space for a sleeping area above. Using glass panels instead of solid walls optimizes light and space.

below Integrating bathing and sitting areas is an unconventional arrangement. However, the orientation of this salvaged bath and sofa adds a degree of separation.

this page Simple white roller blinds modulate and diffuse incoming light from full-width windows, changing the emphasis from the external to the internal environment.

opposite Floor-to-ceiling panels fitted on either side of a bay window add an element of privacy and separation from the busy street outside without reducing light levels.

Positive assets | Converting an interior into a single space means that positive assets, such as ample daylight, an inspiring view or key architectural features are accessible throughout the space, not exclusive to one part of it.

Light enlivens and enhances everything: a plain white wall, the colour and texture of fabric, the shape and line of furniture. It does not simply provide illumination but is a vital asset that can increase a sense of openness and animate a space with contrast and variation. Mapping out the direction in which light enters a space and moves around it, including any bright or dull spots, is essential when planning any structural changes to increase the amount of light in an interior or improve its distribution. This information will help you plan your space to make the most of the available light at different times of day. You may wish to position a sleeping area so you wake up to sunlight, or site a work space to take advantage of late afternoon sun.

If they are an option, extra windows and skylights will let in extra light. Inserting a skylight in a ceiling recess will create a luminous lightwell and a dynamic architectural feature. To diffuse or modulate light in excessively bright environments, or simply to add a degree of separation between internal and external worlds, screen windows or glass walls with removable panels of muslin or wire mesh. Alternatively, fit the ubiquitous roller blinds.

One of the big advantages of living in an open-plan space is the increased general access to and visual prominence of an original or new architectural feature of special interest. In a domestic space, this is often a key architectural feature that was formerly exclusive to one room, such as decorative plaster mouldings on a ceiling, a decorative fireplace, or a large bay window. In an ex-industrial or previously non-domestic environment, original architectural features can act as fascinating reminders of a very different previous existence, and can also become an intrinsic part of a new scheme. For example, a pair of steel loading bay doors might inspire a minimal utilitarian aesthetic, with rough, unfinished walls and exposed surface conduits. Alternatively, a bold new architectural feature, such as a circular skylight, could become the central focus of a space.

However, it is essential to consider the proportion and scale of the architectural features in a new open-plan environment. It is also important to be aware that some original features, such as a period fireplace, which have a powerful link to the previous interior arrangement, may look less impressive or out of place when outside their original framework, consequently undermining the openness and unity of the new arrangement.

opposite An adventurous conversion of a subterranean space maximizes the incoming light entering through a glass ceiling over one half of the space. As the brightest area, this is the logical position for a relaxing zone and an internal garden.

above centre and right A distinctive barrel-vaulted ceiling provided the starting point for this arrangement, with a large kitchen and dining zone occupying the centre and the bathing and sleeping areas arranged all down one side of the space.

Change and review | For some people, one-space living is a logical next step, representing a timely move away from conventional domestic interiors, with their constrictive separations and divisions, towards a versatile and less formal living space. For others, it is something new and challenging; a chance to explore a different way of living, one with a dynamic sense of freedom, space and light.

Before committing yourself to a complete change in lifestyle, think about your circumstances and the level of change you want. Take into account potential developments and changes in the future. Also look at different one-space options. They will provide you with inspiration and information about how to proceed. There are many different ways to embrace the philosophy of open-plan living, and not all of them require a complete rejection of everything that is familiar and recognizable.

If one-space living represents a radical move for you, possibly from a conventional house to a loft conversion, allow for a period of adjustment to this way of life before you undertake alterations or restructuring. Everything is up for review, from how you organize and use your space to the levels of openness and sharing. Even existing furniture may require a rethink. Avoid making any instant decisions. Accept this as a challenge, one that requires a change in attitude and imaginative design and planning solutions, but will lead to a more versatile and practical lifestyle. If making a commitment to this level of change without any previous experience of living in this way concerns you, rent an open-plan space before buying one. It will help you formulate ideas about what you want from a one-space home.

opposite In a New York apartment, flexible curtain track and plastic sheeting separate a sleeping area and diffuse incoming light.

this page This expansive industrial conversion provides opportunities for a series of interconnecting areas. Paper blinds make versatile dividers.

options

BEFORE MAKING ANY CHOICES ABOUT THE SIZE AND TYPE OF SPACE

YOU MOVE INTO, THE OVERALL AESTHETICS AND THE SCALE OF

POSSIBLE STRUCTURAL ALTERATIONS, IT IS ESSENTIAL TO LOOK AT

THE DIFFERENT OPTIONS IN RELATION TO YOUR REQUIREMENTS.

One space opportunities |

There are essentially two different types of one-space home – non-domestic spaces of all descriptions, like ex-industrial units that have undergone a change of use, or conventional properties, such as flats and houses, which are either original open-plan spaces or have been restructured into a single space.

Non-domestic space Ex-light industrial buildings are at a premium in the property market due to their generous proportions and original details. They offer the possibility to develop a new and individual living environment.

Although in theory it is possible to take on such a building and develop it yourself, this is a huge job requiring frequent liaison with local council departments regarding planning permission, change of use (from non-domestic to domestic premises) and the supply of basic utilities. A venture of this kind is a big undertaking and is not without risks. Finding a non-domestic building that can be converted to a single domestic unit is a different matter, one that is worth the time and effort required.

The best option for many buyers is a ready-made conversion. Look for conversions that are sympathetic to the original building, and avoid those that disregard the building and its architecture and have disappointingly conventional interiors as a result. It can be difficult to find units before development, but some developers will allow or even invite input from future purchasers.

If you do see a building of interest undergoing conversion, make enquiries of the builders or developer. Get in on the act of conversion as soon as possible. It is possible to undo new construction work and begin again, but once original details are lost, they are gone forever.

opposite A geometric division of a post-office sorting depot provides distinct activity areas for the artist owner's studio and living space.

above right and right Many non-domestic buildings offer diverse and fascinating options for conversion to single-space homes.

below left A few minor yet effective adjustments brought this 1950s open-plan space up to date to provide a compact and convenient inner-city base.

left and right Removing the partition walls of an earlier conversion restored this space to its original proportions. The kitchen in a cupboard is a tidy solution in a compact space.

Domestic space The benefit of domestic space, in all its incarnations, is its wide availability and a familiar set of references. Often the orientation and proportion of a space is a blueprint copy of other houses or flats of a similar age or style. The interior dimensions, window sizes and ceiling heights are all relatively unchallenging. These details can change with radical restructuring, but even the most inventive schemes cannot conceal the basic framework. And the basic framework of a domestic space is often an immediately recognizable one.

However, many domestic environments have great one-space potential, and there are several options available, ranging from individual houses to purpose-built flats and apartments. Single or two storey buildings are a logical option, especially if there is the potential to improve illumination throughout the space. And while a house extending over three or four different levels is an imperfect option, it is not an unworkable one.

Many flats built since the 1950s already exhibit a degree of open-plan living, integrating day-to-day living activities as an expression of a new informality in contemporary lifestyles. Interestingly, a 1950s flat can impose a stricter sense of architectural correctness than an eighteenth century house. The powerful aesthetics of 1950s, '60s and '70s architecture can dominate a scheme and inhibit a simple rationalization of the space.

As many period houses now exist split into a series of units, reverting a flat-conversion to a single space often restores the interior's original dimensions and reinstates a sense of proportion and light. Windows regain their correct position and light can flow through an interior without the interruption of partition walls.

New aesthetics |

Choosing an aesthetic or an interior style for a single space – whether it is raw and industrial or a sleek precision design with high-specification finishes – will help you to direct your every design and planning decision towards a consistent overall concept. Ideally, consider the aesthetics of your space at the very beginning of a project. Knowing exactly how you want a space to look in the end will provide a vital reference when you are choosing materials to use for flooring and wall finishes, as well as deciding on details such as how to divide and light the space and determining the type of fixtures to install. In this way, the aesthetic becomes an integral part of a space – an attitude or expression of a single style within an interior – not a decorative add-on at the end.

| IDEALLY, CONSIDER THE AESTHETICS OF THE SPACE AT THE VERY BEGINNING OF A PROJECT, NOT AT THE END |

An aesthetic that takes the original architecture of a building as the starting point for a scheme will bring visual definition to a space in a direct and unpretentious way. Conversely, imposing a random aesthetic that has no link to the architecture of a space, unless it is used to present a dynamic and consistent juxtaposition to the interior, will only detract and distract from any sense of unity. This is not a caution against introducing colour, comfort or possessions. All these elements can bring a strong new identity and energy to a scheme. However, it is a caution against an assortment of discordant elements that do not fit together and will diminish an overall sense of space or visual simplicity.

With ex-industrial buildings, such as factories and workshops, a raw, hard-edged aesthetic is in keeping with the original architecture as well as any remaining structural details or industrial elements in the space. Retaining original features is a way of acknowledging

| A MINIMAL, PARED-DOWN AESTHETIC WILL STREAMLINE AN INTERIOR |

the past existence and maintaining the integrity of a space, too. Obliterating any sense of a building's heritage or original purpose by overlayering every surface with a glossy new finish is reckless and insensitive.

In a compact interior, where a sense of space is a key consideration, a minimal, pared-down aesthetic will streamline an interior and optimize space. If this style is to work, orderliness, tidiness and attention to detail are of paramount importance. Vigilance is everything. Edit your possessions and eliminate any redundant items. Clutter or excess furniture will only diminish a sense of space.

Stylistic contrasts between the architecture of a space and its contents can add a sense of excitement to a scheme and animate a space by introducing a degree of friction. Exposed industrial or structural elements and modern upholstered furniture is an interesting combination. Keep to simple, sculptural shapes and a precise symmetrical arrangement of furniture.

Formal or classical domestic architecture often suggests a traditional interior. However, reconfiguring such a space into an open-plan environment equipped with industrial fittings will enliven it with an unexpected element of contradiction. The juxtaposition will be particularly effective if you keep the structural elements and contents apart. Minimize any connections between the two by introducing freestanding fittings and furniture.

right The former sitting room of a large period townhouse was converted into this small single-space apartment. To create a feeling of space and light, the interior has been stripped of its traditional decorative features, leaving a pared-down, minimalist shell.

left Although this space is devoid of decorative objects, the overall design and mix of wood, marble, glass, steel and different planes of white create a visually stimulating yet orderly environment.

above White ceilings and walls and a smooth concrete floor in a voluminous New York loft provide a low-key backdrop to a mix of furniture and artefacts with a strong Eastern influence.

Structural change |

Imaginative planning and design can bring about dramatic spatial transformations and result in the best possible use of the available space and light in an interior. Less radical yet equally inspirational schemes can reorganize space in a way that will provide a convenient and efficient framework for living, fit for current requirements while retaining a degree of flexibility to accommodate future change.

With any level of structural change, basic standards and controls apply, so it is essential to be aware of planning restrictions and to follow any regulations. This is particularly the case with units in a block, historic houses and buildings of special architectural interest, or if you want to make changes to the exterior of a building.

If you remove a structural or load-bearing wall, it is necessary to add a concrete, metal or timber beam to support the opening. The size of the beam depends on how much weight it must support. Knocking through new openings or internal windows, adding mezzanine levels, or removing part of the floor may all require additional support. Some non-domestic buildings can tolerate alterations without requiring additional strengthening. However, it is essential to check with relevant planning departments, a surveyor or a structural engineer before undertaking any structural alterations.

Any reorganization, even the simplest of structural changes, may require changes to the utilities and service systems. They may also be subject to regulations, so seek professional help to assess any alterations and to advise about new systems.

left, above and above right
This bold conversion of a former schoolhouse sensitively juxtaposes new and original features to create a dynamic contemporary environment. The lower floor is a spacious living area with staircases leading to mezzanine levels at each end.

below Hanging from floor to ceiling, paper banners screen off a work area tucked away in a corner and introduce an important element of separation from the main body of the space.

Assessment and action | A pre-condition for action is assessment. Whether you are contemplating low-level alterations or radical change, an objective assessment of your requirements is the essential first step.

The main issues up for review are how best to use the available space, how to integrate different activity zones and how to give visual definition to an overall space. If you live as a couple, a family or a group of individuals, taking into account every individual's requirements in a multi-functional space is a complex process. Yet it will provide you with essential information about your minimum requirements, and indicate any areas that are in need of change or improvement. It will also focus valuable time, effort and creativity into finding workable, economical solutions.

Begin by listing all the different ways in which you use your space. Run through the events of a typical weekday and weekend and list every activity that takes place in your home. Ask yourself which activities are public or social? Which require privacy or isolation? Do conflicts of interest arise as a result of different activities? If you have young children, make two lists for every child, one to cover the child's current requirements and one to cover the child's requirements five years from now.

All this information will indicate ways to organize and combine activities, with different degrees of privacy and openness. It will also provide an essential reference or checklist for any planning or design decisions. Make use of it to keep changes and developments moving in the right direction, in line with your expectations.

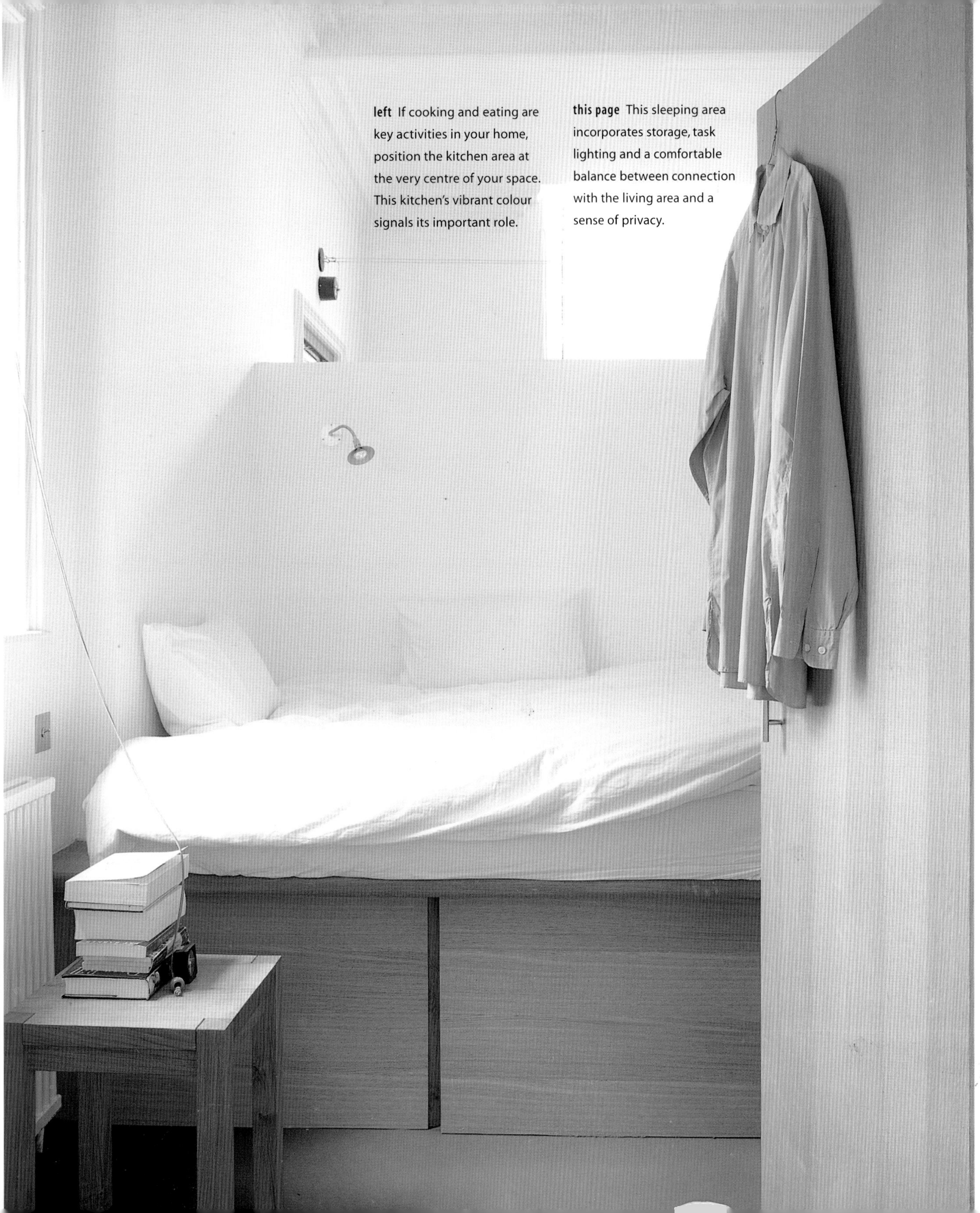

left If cooking and eating are
key activities in your home,
position the kitchen area at
the very centre of your space.
This kitchen's vibrant colour
signals its important role.

this page This sleeping area
incorporates storage, task
lighting and a comfortable
balance between connection
with the living area and a
sense of privacy.

Now that you know exactly what you need from your space, assess it as it currently exists. Include any positive or negative observations about the space. Look closely at the volume and dimensions. Draw a rough floorplan and note the general layout and position of facilities and utilities. Map out circulation routes around the space and note any areas of congestion or inconvenient restrictions. Chart the way that light enters and moves around the space, indicating the different areas that it animates at different times of the day.

Finally, review all the information about your current and future requirements, together with any observations about the space. Before you make any final decisions, take time to think about possible improvements, discuss and review your ideas in depth and investigate every possible option.

Set your budget, find out about any restrictions to possible changes and decide on acceptable levels of disruption and time limits. If you are contemplating structural changes, a major re-organization of space, or changes to existing utilities, this is the moment to bring in professionals for expert advice and creative input.

The end result of assessing every aspect of a project in this way is a clear objective and precise step-by-step plan of action. Regardless of the level of change, aim to find the most practical and economical way ahead. Employing builders, beginning work and then changing tack will increase costs considerably. If at all possible, avoid making any changes to your plans once work is underway. It will save money and potential delays as well as helping you to maintain a good working relationship with your builders.

left A light-industrial space is given an inexpensive makeover with white paint and do-it-yourself structural add-ons including a diagonal division between living and working areas and a step up to a sleeping zone. The result is a simple and comfortable space with a welcoming sense of space, openness and light.

help

FOR COMPLEX PROJECTS OR ALTERATIONS
THAT AFFECT THE BASIC STRUCTURE OF
SERVICES OF A PROPERTY, SOME FORM OF
SPECIALIST GUIDANCE IS ESSENTIAL.

Architects, surveyors, engineers and builders |

Most projects break down into three stages: planning and design, administration and supervision (which includes checking building regulations and applying for planning permissions), and actual building work. For extensive and complex projects, it is important to employ professionals to design, plan and manage the work. For less complex alterations, it is possible to involve experts in only certain aspects of the job – to employ an architect to design and plan the project without overseeing the work, for example. Whatever the size or scale of the job, a professional plan of action will reduce the possibility of mistakes and friction.

Architects An architect brings vision and experience to individual projects, guaranteeing the best possible result in terms of creativity and cost-efficiency. As well as planning and design, an architect can suggest or select materials, find specialist contractors and manufacturers to provide individual fixtures and fittings, and recommend a good builder. The basis of a good working relationship is trust, communication and confidence, so meet and talk with architects whose work you like, or ask friends for recommendations. Ask to see photographs of recent projects, or go and visit them yourself.

Chartered surveyors Chartered surveyors offer advice on all aspects of buying and selling property. If you are contemplating buying a property or making structural changes to your current property, a building survey will provide essential information about the condition of the building. It will point out any defects, which may influence your decision to buy, or indicate areas that are in need of improvement and development.

Structural engineers Structural engineers will assess a building's structure and stability. Areas for consideration include the foundations, walls, columns, beams and roof components – all relevant to every aspect of building design, construction, repair, conversion and extension. A structural engineer can specify materials, prepare technical drawings, check regulations and restrictions and obtain relevant consents and permissions, prepare costings and monitor the actual building work.

Builders The best option for finding a builder is personal recommendation. If you are employing an architect or a structural engineer, they will be able to find or suggest builders to undertake your work. Alternatively, trade associations can recommend local builders. Be precise about your requirements – prepare a detailed written brief and ask the builder for a written estimate.

belgian beach house

CASE STUDY 1 | SPACIOUS SEASIDE APARTMENT

This radical architectural transformation of a contemporary yet conventional weekend home in a coastal town allows the owners maximum flexibility. The new open-plan scheme significantly improves the use of space, light distribution and access to sea views. Now a translucent environment with a sense of spaciousness and freedom that is entirely in keeping with its seaside location, the apartment offers a refreshing escape from the complexities of urban life.

In an ideal location overlooking the sea, this apartment is a long rectangular space that runs the full length of an uninspiring purpose-built block, with expansive windows and outdoor terraces at either end. Standard windows ranged down one side of the space look out on to an identical building next door. The original interior, an unimaginative domestic layout with inadequate light distribution and restricted sea views, did not optimize the positive assets of the space.

The architects' new scheme comprises large open areas at both ends of the apartment, which make good use of the wonderful light and sea views. At the front of the apartment, a spacious sitting, dining and kitchen area overlooks the sea, while at the back, the sleeping area faces towards the town. A sequence of individual work, storage, shower and bathing areas line up in between, connecting the two ends of the apartment.

Moving panels of opaque glass and wood provide multiple possibilities for opening or enclosing every area and subdividing the space as a whole. A wooden panel that slides across the corridor splits the apartment into two sections, while a glass panel in a similar position produces a very different degree of separation. The moving panels underline and facilitate the architects' intention to provide flexible, optional divisions between a front-of-house area and back-of-house facilities. And

floor plan This modern seaside apartment consists of a long, thin rectangular space with large windows at either end and all along one outside wall. Versatile sliding panels divide the front and back of the apartment into two distinct zones, public and private, with additional subdivisions for working, bathing and storage areas sandwiched in between.

sleeping

bathing

bathing   working   cooking

dining   relaxing

opposite inset left and right The kitchen area is a series of flexible divisions, from the stainless steel shutter that screens the work surface and appliances to the movable glass panels that enclose it.

this page A corridor running the length of the apartment links the main sleeping and living areas. Wood or glass panels can slide across the corridor to create a sense of separation.

while the new organization of space retains an element of the original layout, with the sitting and kitchen areas on the sea side and sleeping and bathing on the town side, the experience of being in the space is radically different.

Surrounding the kitchen area with glass panels continues the principle of flexibility. When closed, the panels create an opaque box, like an abstract art installation. As panels open or slide, the area reconfigures, and sightlines and access change. Four independent panels facing the sea pivot inwards or outwards in multiple variations, reflecting and refracting light with their every movement. Each glass panel projects monochromatic images and shadows, enlivening the space with a new landscape and extra dimensions.

opposite above The sleeping area is a secondary relaxing zone, with comfortable furniture, a television and different lighting options.

opposite below Stacking tables are a flexible alternative to traditional bedside furniture.

main picture A perfect relaxing zone, complete with natural light, variable heating, soft seating and a low table for drinks or books.

right and inset right A desk fitted into a narrow alcove provides a useful work space.

Other reflective surfaces throughout the space catch and throw back light and shadows with similar effect. The sycamore flooring running from front to back (except in the shower and bathing areas), the stainless steel kitchen worktops, equipment and shuttering and the expansive mirrors all contribute to a general effect of luminosity and a special quality of light.

White roller blinds at every window moderate the amount of incoming light, reduce glare or heat and maintain a temperate environment. Altering the position of the blinds also alters the focus of the space. With the blinds down, the light is diffused and a sense of enclosure and refuge is created. When the blinds are up, revealing views of the ever-changing sea and sky, there is a sense of exposure to the elements and connection with the world outside.

zoning

relaxing | cooking | bathing | sleeping | working

this page In a light, open workshop conversion, a high-level storage panel in the kitchen area separates front-of-house and back-of-house activities.

ORGANIZING A SINGLE SPACE IS ABOUT COMBINING DIFFERENT ACTIVITIES INTO A LOGICAL SEQUENCE OF INTERCONNECTING ZONES. DESIGNATING A WELL-LIT, OPEN AREA AS A RELAXING ZONE WILL PROVIDE A WELCOMING ENVIRONMENT, SOMEWHERE TO BE AT EASE WITH FAMILY AND FRIENDS.

relaxing

A single space incorporates many different activities. Dividing these activities into zones facilitates good organization and the optimum use of space. Few zones are dedicated to a single activity – the majority combine several related activities, such as cooking and eating or reading and listening to music. Unlike a conventional domestic environment, which has set divisions between different zones, an open-plan environment is about freedom, flexibility and integration. So the way a zone relates to the general space is just as important as the way it functions in its own right.

There is no set formula for organizing zones within a space – everyone has different requirements and every space will suggest a different solution. For example, if you enjoy social activities such as cooking, eating and sitting around the table talking with friends and family, this suggests one way to organize your

left A sliding panel provides an ingenious flexible storage solution for a multi-functional relaxing zone and adds a block of vibrant colour to a light, white space.

above Chairs grouped beside a window create a welcoming and sociable spot. Lightweight folding chairs are easy to reconfigure in different arrangements or to store flat.

space. If you enjoy other pursuits, such as watching videos, listening to music and playing a flute, this suggests a different arrangement.

Ideally, take advantage of well-lit areas for your relaxing, eating and cooking zones. The proportion of space and prominence given to each activity is a matter of individual preference. It is important to assess your personal requirements and organize the main living area to fit in with your lifestyle.

In a typical multi-functional relaxing zone, where many activities coexist and overlap, a flexible arrangement of furniture, storage and lighting is essential. The style and position of furniture and the lighting effects go a long way towards defining and facilitating everyday use and enjoyment of the zone.

When choosing furniture, consider the scale and architecture of your interior. In an expansive loft, for example, a geometric arrangement of big sofas and a central low table will anchor a relaxing zone. Soft textures and shapes can provide an interesting juxtaposition with industrial concrete flooring or other non-domestic details. In smaller environments, beware of allowing oversized pieces to dominate the space, as they may compromise the overall flexibility and versatility of the zone.

A configuration of chairs is often the main indicator of a relaxing zone, establishing a general style and indicating the level of informality. Different chairs fit different activities, so aim to provide a selection of soft (easy) and hard (upright) seating

opposite far left A fabric tent defines an intimate alternative seating arrangement for breakfast and afternoon tea.

opposite above and below Simple muslin drapes diffuse sunlight and provide semi-transparent dividers between public and private areas.

this page The classic style and formal arrangement of the table and chairs contrasts with the raw structure of a New York loft space.

to meet your requirements and to define different activities. For example, group armchairs together for conversation and lounging, position a recliner on its own for quiet reading, and gather more upright chairs together around a table for eating. Sofas often end up as a big seat for one person, so do not automatically include a sofa. If you enjoy stretching out and putting your feet up, a chaise longue or daybed may be a better option, as they take up less space and are often more comfortable. On a practical note, single chairs are easier to move and reconfigure into different seating arrangements and therefore are more versatile.

A selection of low stools and storage cubes make space-efficient supplementary seating – ideal for the occasional influx of people – and also function as mini tables for the phone, a pile of books or a coffee cup. Floor cushions can add extra comfort and an informal note, as well as providing child-friendly seating options.

this page In a typical multi-functional living space, arrangements of furniture and lighting suggest different activities. A classic sofa, low table and task lighting provide a comfortable place for reading and relaxing.

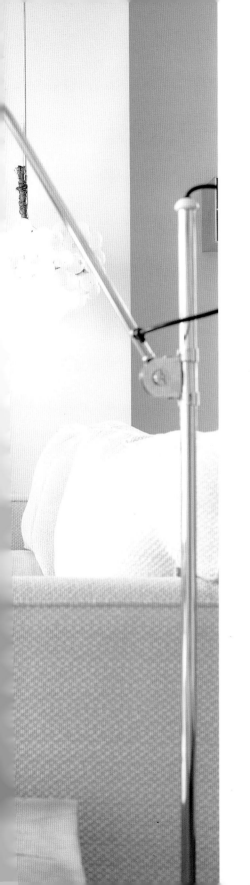

As an inexpensive alternative to classic or contemporary chairs, a bed can provide a comfortable communal seating platform and works well in either a big space or a small studio. Choose a bed base on wheels for maximum flexibility. Throw on a cover to protect and conceal bedlinen. Store pillows and duvet elsewhere or, if the bed is high enough, in boxes beneath it. Some divans come with built-in storage space in the base.

Accessible and flexible storage solutions will help create a sense of organization and maintain a sense of space. Books, television sets, CD players, CDs, video recorders, video cassettes, board and computer games, and any other special interest items such as musical instruments

opposite far left In an open-plan apartment, a table and chairs in a quiet setting by a window provide an alternative to the main dining table.

above A narrow architectural recess off the main living space is furnished with easy chairs and a soft rug to provide an intimate and informal seating area.

below left A mobile trolley allows a television and video to be wheeled into position for easy viewing and stored out of sight when not in use.

below centre Wooden-frame chairs with woven seats, like these contemporary classics, provide comfort without taking up much space and are easy to move into different seating arrangements.

below right Somewhere to sit away from the main living area, like these chairs and table in an upstairs gallery, offers an alternative setting for peaceful relaxation.

all require shelf space. Finding a place for everything is a challenge, but designing and putting together efficient storage options will go a long way towards alleviating conflicts of interest and potential chaos. However, if everything is hidden from view an area can look austere and unwelcoming. Strike a balance – display favourite items and store the rest out of sight.

Mobile trolleys are a big bonus in a one-space environment, enabling you to move heavy pieces of entertainment equipment around easily and relocate them when they are not in use. For example, you can push a large-screen television into a central area for viewing then wheel it out of sight afterwards.

Some storage solutions are architectural or take advantage of the structure of a space to provide inventive options. Fitting a bookcase into a narrow recess makes use of an otherwise empty space and provides

unobtrusive storage. Exploit architectural quirks and make the most of alcoves or recesses by using them to house storage units or display space.

Creative lighting is an important factor in a relaxing zone. Different combinations of lights signal different moods, from bright and upbeat to low-key and intimate. Subtle ambient lighting is ideal for relaxing and entertaining and a simple dimmer switch on a central fitting can deliver this effect. Accent lighting will enliven an environment by introducing contrasting areas of light and shade, while task lighting will direct a pool of light to illuminate a specific activity.

Lighting design is a complex issue. If you plan to install a new lighting system, then consult an expert. However, investing in floor lights to supplement a basic installation of central fittings and wall lights will provide scope for many different combinations.

this page An expansive double-height picture window in a New York loft makes a compelling backdrop to a comfortable seating area.

london purpose built

CASE STUDY 2 | MODERN CITY APARTMENT

This compact modern apartment is only a few

minutes' walk away from the owner's design studio.

A powerful architectural aesthetic combined with the

convenience and advantages of a buzzing inner-city

location makes this small space an inspiring yet

functional base. Several ingenious alterations have

successfully revitalized and updated the space by

acknowledging the spirit and integrity of the original

concept without creating a set piece of design history.

This apartment, one of a series of open-plan single or double occupancy units, is situated on the top floor of a low-rise block in an inner-city location. The block is part of a 1950s council-housing complex built for local blue-collar professionals such as nurses and the police.

With a Grade II listing to protect the existing space and limit any changes, acknowledging and understanding the history of the apartment is an important part of the owner/occupier package and adds to the excitement of living here – even though regulations and restrictions sometimes protect the wrong thing, like an unauthentic replacement kitchen. So while the owner's ambition is restoration, even returning the kitchen to something like its original simplicity now requires planning permission.

The apartment's full-width arched window and barrel-shaped ceiling are exclusive to the top-floor units in the block and contribute to the high levels of light and general sense of space. The wall of glass outlines a

this page and opposite The view from the entrance shows the kitchen area at the left, sitting area directly ahead, and the sleeping area within an open box to the right.

panoramic view of east London. This view, and an overall impression of luminosity and space, are the first things that strike you upon entering the apartment, drawing the eye past the kitchen area set to one side of the entrance and into the main living area beyond.

Seventy per cent of the space is occupied by a living area that contains different seating configurations that define different activities. There are chairs arranged around a table for eating or working, chairs positioned

right Dividing the kitchen and the main living area is the original storage system, with a combination of open and solid-back shelving. It efficiently accommodates the typical assortment of kitchen paraphernalia as well as effectively screening any disorder from view.

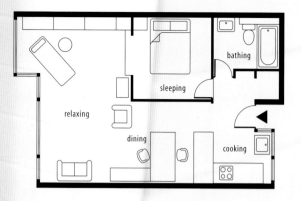

floor plan The apartment is a compact rectangular shape, with a wall of glass situated in front of the relaxing zone. A barrel-shaped ceiling links arched windows at the back and front of the space.

Attention to detail on the part of the original architects means that there are several useful open storage solutions built into the kichen and relaxing areas – vital in a space of this size.

for contemplating the view from the window and a group configuration with a sofa for conversation and socializing. A solitary lounger, reading light and occasional table together with a large collection of design and photographic books signal the key area of interest and activity. The simple storage system for books is one of the new additions to the space. Running the full length of the living area, the shelving provides an opportunity for both storage and display.

In full view from the lounger, the sleeping zone is an open box one step up from the main living area. The change in level, a wall panel intersecting the storage unit and the chain curtain are all new additions. The wall and the chain divider provide an ingenious division between areas without compromising ease of transition or the sense of overall openness. They underline what is remarkable about this compact space. Different areas interconnect in a logical sequence, yet also manage to convey a sense of independence and change in style specific to their different functions.

left and above right Hanging a chain-link curtain across the opening between the main sitting area and sleeping zone provides an inventive screen.

above left A shelving tower provides storage for shirts and can be spun round to face the wall, leaving a single shelf on view for bedside items.

below left and right Open storage for books, with sliding aluminium panels to break up the display, continues right into the sleeping area.

WITH RESOURCEFUL PLANNING IT IS POSSIBLE TO DESIGN A HIGH-PERFORMANCE, USER-FRIENDLY KITCHEN AREA. CLEVER DIVIDERS AND GOOD STORAGE WILL ADD FLEXIBILITY AND VERSATILITY AND FACILITATE INTEGRATION WITH THE REST OF YOUR SPACE.

cooking

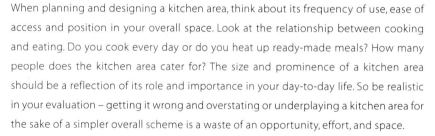

When planning and designing a kitchen area, think about its frequency of use, ease of access and position in your overall space. Look at the relationship between cooking and eating. Do you cook every day or do you heat up ready-made meals? How many people does the kitchen area cater for? The size and prominence of a kitchen area should be a reflection of its role and importance in your day-to-day life. So be realistic in your evaluation – getting it wrong and overstating or underplaying a kitchen area for the sake of a simpler overall scheme is a waste of an opportunity, effort, and space.

Before you decide to rearrange your space to accommodate a new kitchen area or change around an existing installation, it is vital to check utilities and services. Water supplies and drainage are essential services that require access to external walls. It is possible to update or extend existing systems to allow a change in position of a kitchen area, although if a system is deficient or out of date, a complete refit is the best option. Always get professional advice to work out the most practical, cost-efficient option.

above left Precision fixtures and fittings, like these high-specification stainless steel units, utensils and worktops, create a minimalist look.

above A capsule kitchen can be hidden away behind folding and retractable doors.

opposite In a city apartment used for weekend breaks, this compact, utilitarian kitchen-in-a-cupboard is exactly the right size for use.

above top and bottom Clever ideas like fitting an oven in the end of a table and slotting in a fridge beneath steps to a mezzanine level maximize space in a compact and minimalist kitchen area.

above Long wooden benches, which can be neatly tucked away beneath the table when not in use, are a space-saving seating solution that is ideally suited to this simple and clutter-free cooking zone.

opposite above left and right Tall windows on two sides of the kitchen area illuminate food preparation and eating areas. The Venetian blinds modulate incoming light, preventing glare.

opposite below Integrating a high-specification food preparation area, complete with two-ring hob and circular kitchen sink, with a kitchen table, is an ingenious use of the available space.

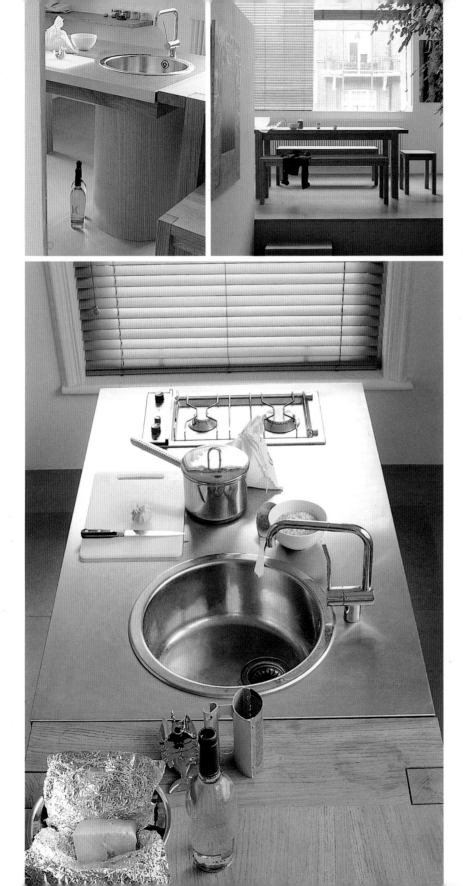

Drainage and waste pipes require a minimum gradient, so aim to place any kitchen sinks, dishwashers and washing machines within a reasonable distance of an external outlet. Ideally, plan new piping or extensions to existing pipes with as few twists and bends as possible to reduce any risk of blockages.

Good ventilation removes excess moisture from the atmosphere and prevents cooking smells from invading the rest of the space – this is a valid precaution if, for example, clothes are kept in an open storage system. Open windows go a long way to keep fresh air circulating, yet high-specification cooking equipment can produce excessive amounts of moisture that will damage and discolour the fabric of an environment. And while smell is a powerful and vital stimulant in the preparation, cooking and eating process, the lingering smell of yesterday's food is not quite as appealing. However, a quick session with an extractor fan or ventilation system will soon clear the air. For direct and immediate effect, install an extractor unit above cooking equipment or, to provide good general ventilation, fit extractor fans in walls and windows.

Orientation is an important factor within the kitchen area itself and affects its integration with the overall space. For example, fitting a low-level line of equipment and units along a perimeter wall, possibly with a window and view outside, focuses a kitchen area, and anyone working in it, away from the rest of the space. Standing at a work surface preparing food or cooking involves turning your back on everything else. If you like to work away from any distraction, possibly in isolation, then this is a good option.

Fitting an identical arrangement of low-level equipment and units away from the wall, with access from both sides so people can walk around the unit easily and freely, will simply transform the orientation of your kitchen area and the experience of being in it. If you live with young children who require your attention,

or like cooking to be a social event, then this is a practical and accessible arrangement. Likewise, dividing a kitchen into two parallel lines – perhaps one high-level and one low-level – or locating everything in a central unit or block, will involve different movements around the kitchen area and create different connections and interaction with the overall space.

If your kitchen area is also intended to be a social place take this into account in the general planning and design. Include broad work surfaces with access from both sides and put stools around a work-table to positively encourage people to participate or spectate. Alternatively, provide somewhere comfortable where they can sit close by but away from the general work traffic. A sense of openness, easy access and light will all promote the kitchen area as a friendly, welcoming environment.

Pay attention to safety issues. Do not invite people to sit next to a hazardous hot surface. Keep seating away from the main work triangle between cooking unit, sink and work surface. And for general efficiency and safety, incorporate heat-proof surfaces alongside cooking units so the cook can avoid walking around with hot pots and pans.

above left Providing a place to sit, like these swivel chairs attached to the end of a worktop, signal the kitchen area as a social place.

main picture Parallel high- and low-level cabinets accommodate an efficient kitchen with easy access to the ample storage space.

above For an inexpensive yet individual kitchen design, use standard drawers, cupboards and units but fit new front panels.

below Power sockets set flush in a worktop facilitate efficiency and convenience and avoid the hazard of trailing power leads.

above Two sliding panels at
the end of this kitchen area
provide varying degrees of
separation and modulate light.
When fully open, they align
with a vertical storage unit at
the end of the kitchen area.

opposite above In a converted
former school-house, the
compact kitchen area is
slotted in neatly beneath
a mezzanine level and
overlooks a double-height
eating and relaxing zone.

opposite right Flat panels that
flip down to hide appliances
and a food preparation area,
and a roller blind between
the kitchen and eating areas,
screen the kitchen area itself
as well as any disorder.

Apart from fitting a cooking unit and sink (for obvious safety and technical reasons), there is no reason to permanently fix anything else in one place. Mobile work surfaces, kitchen tables and storage units will all add versatility to a kitchen area and make your working environment responsive to changing requirements. Even in a compact kitchen area, including a single mobile unit and storing it out of the way under a work surface or in a built-in cupboard will increase flexibility.

Creating a kitchen with different, varying levels of enclosure and openness also increases flexibility and versatility. Simple ideas like a pull-down shutter or sliding screen to enclose a cooking unit can shift the focus of a kitchen area away from the function of preparing large family meals to simple low-key activities like making a single cup of coffee. This change in emphasis and appearance introduces new possibilities for use, changing the dynamic from that of a hard-working area to a more low-key and informal one. Alternatively, use lighting to transfer emphasis from one activity area to another.

Streamlining the industrial elements of a kitchen area into a single panel or unit can add efficiency and visual simplicity to an arrangement. Planning a kitchen area as a series of logical and ergonomic workstations, perhaps with one low-level and one high-level unit, will optimize the available space. One solution to a small space is to integrate cooking and eating areas into a single central workbench, with an oven and hob built in at one end and a separate

left and below In a remarkably compact kitchen area, a glass panel fixed over the stairwell is a clever idea that allows light to penetrate the depths of the staircase and creates an additional worksurface. Open shelves and wall-mounted plate racks provide accessible extra storage space.

right An ingenious custom-built folding table with an extending base offers a choice of table lengths and when not in use stores away flat in a recess in the wall.

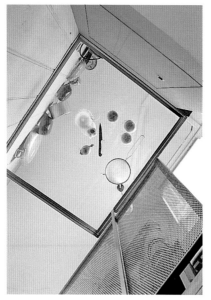

storage unit elsewhere. This approach does not preclude display and open storage, which can add vitality and individuality to an area, but it is a caution against overcrowding or clutter.

Keep an open mind about the layout and aesthetics of a kitchen until you finalize its location and structure. While thinking about how you will organize the area is a critical part of the decision-making process, setting your heart on an industrial aesthetic, with stainless steel equipment and work surfaces, may not be the best solution for integrating the area into the rest of your space. Sometimes the best option is a compromise of aesthetics, cost-efficiency and practicality. Taking an overview is essential in an open-plan environment and an efficient scheme that makes good use of space is far preferable to an unworkable or over-complex arrangement of set pieces.

Choose fittings and equipment that are compatible with the scale and general style of the interior. Standard fixtures and fittings can look out of scale in a loft space – this type of environment offers an opportunity to use bold architectural statements and unconventional elements, such as concrete work surfaces and industrial-style lighting. In a compact space, choose sleek precision elements to maximize the available space. Slim dishwashers and washing machines offer useful alternatives to standard-width equipment and can make all the difference between an efficient area and a labour-intensive one.

this page Open shelving suspended in front of a window creates storage space for pots and pans and adds a bold visual focus in a compact galley-style kitchen.

london industrial unit

Converting a raw industrial unit to domestic use is an exciting opportunity to devise an original and individual place to live. Taking on a project of this size and complexity, co-ordinating and designing every aspect personally without any previous experience, as the owner of this space did, and producing such an uncompromisingly modern scheme, is a triumph of vision and determination.

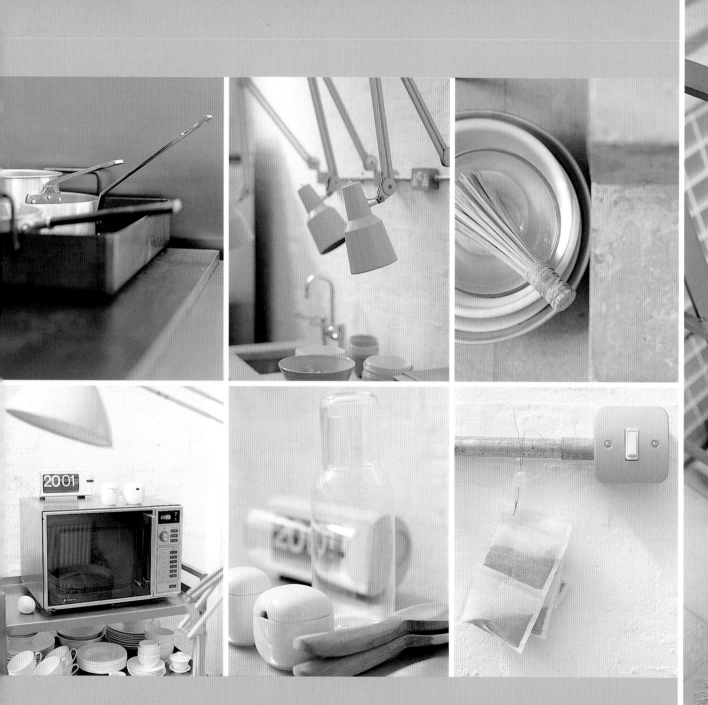

this page above Many of the kitchen fittings are industrial. The anglepoise lamps are ex-hospital fixtures and bring a laboratory aesthetic to the food-preparation area.

this page below Everyday items are kept close at hand. Along with an assortment of other utensils, a set of plain white china is stacked on a second-hand catering trolley.

right Part of the upper level is cut away to provide access and light to the lower level, making it possible to stand in the living area and look down into the kitchen below.

This exceptional apartment was once part of a printing works in London's East End. The owner bought an empty space on two levels with no existing connections, just rough concrete floors, bare brick walls, large windows on the upper level, inadequate light on the lower level and no basic utilities. After conversion this industrial unit is now a unique home and work space for the owner, a food writer and art director, and his partner. Given the professional food angle, the style and position of the kitchen is a big factor in the scheme of things.

Initial plans sited the kitchen area on the upper level, at the end of the main living space alongside the original loading-bay doors, to allow street-level access after food shopping. However, the owner decided against installing a kitchen in full view of the main living area, where it would be the visual focus of the space, instead allocating it a key position of power and significance on the lower level. After a radical spatial reworking, including the removal of part of the floor on the upper level and the insertion of a glass walkway and connecting stairway to the lower level, the kitchen is the new centre of the space, with all other areas radiating outwards from this magnetic core.

The kitchen area encapsulates the industrial aesthetic running throughout the space. It is all steel and concrete, with a battery of expensive professional catering equipment built in alongside more eclectic freestanding second-hand finds and salvaged pieces. Despite the absence of colour, except during food preparation, it is still a vibrant and visually stimulating area. When viewed from the gallery in the main living area above, the kitchen looks welcoming yet low-key.

An external door at the top of a flight of stairs from the basement, one of four separate entrances to the unit, provides access after food shopping trips. Other hidden assets tucked away behind the kitchen area include structural alcoves and cave-like storage spaces

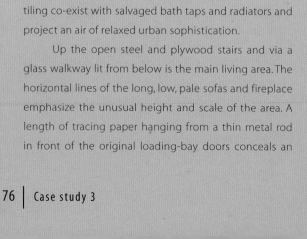

above A low horizontal opening in the wall forms an unusual lateral fireplace that emphasizes the spaciousness of the sitting area and provides a focal point.

above Recessed shapes set into the thickness of one wall and individually lit in different colours provide display and storage space as well as architectural interest.

that provide a generous pantry and scullery. Small-scale areas like these offset the expansiveness of the general space and add an essential element of intimacy.

The sleeping area connects to the kitchen via a glass dividing wall and sliding clear glass panel. And beyond the sleeping area, behind a wooden panel, are a bath and shower. Here again, witty juxtapositions add vitality to the scheme. High-specification fixtures and fittings like underfloor heating and wall-to-wall mosaic tiling co-exist with salvaged bath taps and radiators and project an air of relaxed urban sophistication.

Up the open steel and plywood stairs and via a glass walkway lit from below is the main living area. The horizontal lines of the long, low, pale sofas and fireplace emphasize the unusual height and scale of the area. A length of tracing paper hanging from a thin metal rod in front of the original loading-bay doors conceals an original yet unpopular architectural feature. The paper diffuses light, reduces the view of a development site opposite and screens the interior from passers-by.

Except for the mosaic tiles in the bath and shower area, the flooring throughout the space is concrete paving slabs. Three applications of sealant were applied to protect the highly absorbent surface from spills and damage. High-specification underfloor heating takes the edge and chill off this modest element – yet another juxtaposition of exclusive and low-budget elements in this dramatic and unpretentious conversion.

left The soft outlines of second-hand sofas offset the new elemental concrete floors and walls and present an upbeat interpretation of a traditional lounge area.

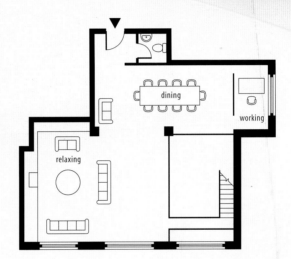

floor plan The space is situated on two levels with part of the upper level cut away to allow light into the basement level. Cast concrete steps with plywood treads connect the two different levels and lead via a glass walkway from the sitting area down into the kitchen area.

opposite above left In keeping with the industrial aesthetic, a sheet of mirror leans up against the back of the iroko wood divider between the bathing and sleeping areas.

opposite above right Unlike standard bathroom fittings, the scale and functional designs of hospital or laboratory taps fit in perfectly with the dimensions of an industrial conversion.

opposite below left and right The monumental panel of iroko wood that divides the sleeping and bathing areas also acts as a headboard for the bed. The intense colour of the wood provides a dramatic contrast to the pale blue mosaic tiles that line the bathing zone beyond.

right The bathing area boldly incorporates a number of salvaged fixtures and fittings, yet the ample light and space, and warmth from underfloor heating pipes, create an underlying sense of luxury.

main picture Sliding panels of textured glass divide an informal family bathing zone from the main sleeping area.

right A solid panel that is housed in a recess in the wall can be swung across the corridor to divide public and private areas.

COMMUNAL OR SEPARATE, COLOURFUL OR LOW-KEY, HIGH-TECH OR FUNCTIONAL – PLANNING A BATHING AREA IS ABOUT FINDING A SOLUTION THAT OPTIMIZES SPACE AND FITS IN WITH YOUR LIFESTYLE.

bathing

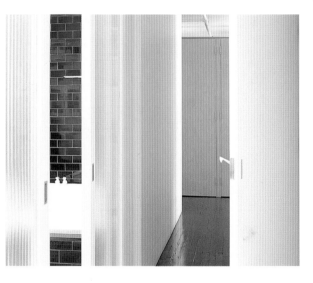

A bathing area is a place where you will be naked and accordingly at your most vulnerable. Assess how you feel about this in terms of providing an open or possibly communal bathing area – it may be that some degree of enclosure and separation is an essential practical concession. If communal bathing and showering is acceptable to you and your family, yet the lavatory is one area requiring enclosure, then design and plan your bathing zone accordingly or provide a separate lavatory in a different location. Direct access to a lavatory is preferable to walking past the bath or walking through a shower room, and avoids outdoor shoe traffic crossing clean, or possibly wet, flooring.

this page A combination of colours, textures and shapes enlivens this spacious communal bathing area in a New York loft.

this page A sculptural, curving wall screens a small bathing zone. Access to the shower is by the window, while at the opposite end of the wall is the door to a separate lavatory.

If you share a bathing zone, especially with young children, consider the many different requirements and schedules that will govern its use. In a family, the mornings are often peak or even crisis time. Everyone is showering or cleaning teeth together or in quick succession. Providing an extra shower room or lavatory will reduce congestion and possible friction first thing in the morning. Even if you live alone, there will be times when guests are staying and competing with you for the facilities. A separate lavatory is useful if your bathing and sleeping zones are integrated, as it provides a place for visitors to use and directs general traffic away from a potentially private area.

It is logical to integrate sleeping and bathing zones in some way and provide a sense of division or separation from the rest of your space. Possibly divide your interior into open and public front-of-house space, containing the relaxing, cooking and eating zones, and private back-of-house space for sleeping and bathing zones. The layout of your space may naturally suggest a degree of separation – perhaps locating sleeping and bathing zones on a mezzanine level, or at one end of the property. A sliding or moving panel can reinforce this sense of division as well as providing privacy, reducing noise transference and maintaining a comfortable and constant temperature.

Creating a solid division between public and private zones, possibly a wood or plasterboard sliding or fixed panel, demarcates space effectively. A division of this kind provides an opportunity for greater freedom and openness in planning and designing sleeping and bathing zones. For a family, this option also presents an opportunity for a more informal private zone layout with communal relaxation and play areas.

Glass screens and sliding doors fit in well with the functional aspect of bathing zones. Opaque or textured glass makes an ideal divider between sleeping and bathing areas and offers the advantage of privacy and enclosure without the disadvantage of blocking light. If visibility is a sensitive issue, beware of installing opaque glass:

above and left The wall of waterproof plaster curls around the small shower and screens it from the main sleeping area without entirely separating the two zones.

right and far right These sleeping and showering areas are divided by a partition wall that includes an unobtrusive strip window which allows natural light to filter into the internal shower room.

it is less opaque when wet, so condensation and shower spray will affect its transparency. Also, it is less effective as a screen if it is in close proximity to whatever it is screening. However, for wonderful light diffusion and pure luminosity it is worth making a few exceptions.

Fabric dividers like muslin or voile provide an inexpensive and atmospheric enclosure for a bath and define a place for relaxation and revitalization. Warmth, low-key lighting and a sense of stillness will aid this essential process. Orientate a bath towards a window for a restful view of trees and sky. Or use aromatic candles to counterbalance a clinical or functional aesthetic and change the dynamic of a space. Install a dimmer control on artificial lights and use low-level lighting to signal a change in pace and aid relaxation.

Take into account the structure and dimensions of a bathing zone and its overall aesthetic when choosing fittings and fixtures. For example, an imaginative, space-saving minuscule shower and basin capsule requires high-specification compact fixtures and fittings that are in line with the general effect of streamlining and

above left and main picture Semi-transparent muslin drapes divide this bathing and sitting area but still allow a strong sense of connection and openness between the two zones.

above A collection of pebbles and sponges in the bottom of the bath make an appealing display. Pumice stone is both decorative and practical.

opposite A salvaged period bath with a flaking, worn surface provides a functional yet decorative focal point in this unpretentious scheme.

above A wall of folding panels open and close to reveal and conceal a capsule bathing area with a shower enclosure slotted neatly beyond.

left and far left High-specification fixtures and fittings optimize space in a compact shower enclosure. Horizontal bars set over a vertical radiator make a practical towel rail.

opposite above Make the most of high ceilings by creating platforms or mezzanine levels. Here, a sleeping platform is stacked on top of a bathing area.

opposite below Situated under the sleeping platform, this small bathing area has no direct source of light, so relies on a glazed internal window to increase light levels.

efficiency. Simple and precise elements like mixer taps, a built-in storage unit and a rigid shower-head work well in this type of environment.

At the opposite end of the scale, a conversion of a former industrial space with raw brickwork and surface piping requires bold and generous fixtures and fittings that are in keeping with the no-fuss utilitarian aesthetic. A concrete bath with mosaic tiling and a huge salvaged shower-head that projects water on to a sloping floor are appropriate choices, in proportion with the original industrial fittings throughout the space.

Unconventional fixtures and fittings can provide unpretentious and inexpensive alternatives to standard products. Laboratory taps, basins and medicine cabinets create a clinical effect and guarantee reliable, long-term performance. Shop display or hotel fittings, such as combination hooks for clothing, extending rails and metal shelving, offer hard-working storage space for accessories and towels. Commercial kitchen suppliers offer lots of inspiration and inexpensive products. Stainless steel sinks and tubs, ceramic hand-basins for professional kitchens, and metal and plastic storage bins all transfer easily into a domestic bathing zone.

If you plan to use standard fixtures and fittings, opt for simple shapes in white. Introduce colour, texture, or contrast with flooring, tiles, or paint. A one-off item like a Japanese-style cedar bath, wooden basin or a simple bamboo mat adds organic warmth and texture. Contrasts between textures and materials, such as wood and ceramic, or concrete and glass, will enliven a potentially uniform area.

Architectural devices, like a curving dividing wall between a bathing and sleeping zone, a round shower enclosure or an opaque glass screen, will offset any clinical hard edges with sculptural forms and shadows. Simple yet inventive details along these lines add individuality within a bathing zone and, if visible from outside, present a new perspective to the overall space.

SLEEP IS A VITAL AND RESTORATIVE ACTIVITY. WHETHER YOU
DEDICATE A PROMINENT AREA TO YOUR SLEEPING ZONE OR SIMPLY
INSTALL A FOLD-UP BED, PROVIDING A COMFORTABLE AND RESTFUL
ENVIRONMENT IS ESSENTIAL FOR INDIVIDUAL WELL-BEING.

sleeping

left In an expansive New York loft, oriental screens and muslin drapes divide a sleeping area from the main space and provide texture and contrast to the raw industrial infrastructure.

right A muslin tent transforms a simple pine bed into an intimate retreat and adds a final layer of separation within a sleeping zone.

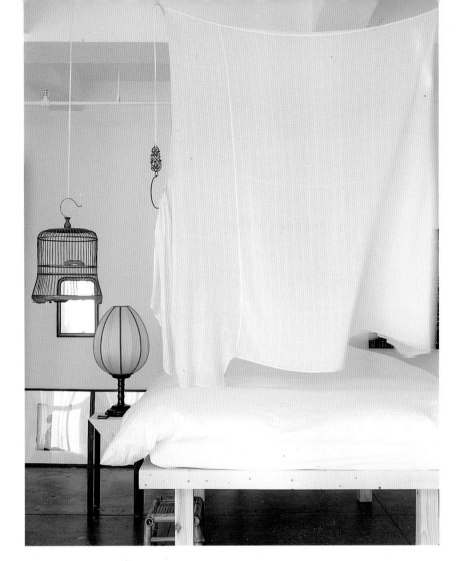

Light is a big factor when allocating an area for sleep. Depending on your personal preference, waking up to bright morning light is either an invigorating experience or an unwelcome one. If access to direct light is important to you, then orientate a sleeping area towards a window or under a skylight. If morning light is not a priority then save the good light option for another zone, perhaps cooking or relaxing.

Dedicating a zone to sleeping is a wonderful opportunity to create a retreat from the outside world and provide ideal conditions for a good rest. If you share your life with a partner, children or friends, any time alone is a precious event. A sleeping zone that offers a degree of separation can offer the perfect haven for a vital restorative or contemplative episode at any time of the day.

Building a high bed base can add to a general sense of separation and isolation, while a lightweight fabric tent draped around a bed will reduce noise and at the same time provide a degree of privacy. Alternatively, hang fabric dividers, or even paper banners, as an effective barrier between a bed and the adjacent zone. This is a simple device that focuses attention on the bed in the sleeping zone

left and above Reducing the height of an internal wall to provide a support for a metal sleeping platform provides an inventive sleeping area in an attic apartment. When positioning a platform, consider the amount of space remaining above and below. This is a critical measurement that affects ease of use and comfort. Ideally, allow standing room on the platform. If this makes the platform too low, use the area beneath it as storage space.

while concealing it from the rest of the open-plan environment. If space is limited, dedicating a separate area to sleeping is not always an option. Combining a sleeping zone with a different yet compatible activity is one solution and is a good way to make the most of the available space. Alternatively, inserting a mezzanine level or sleeping platform will provide an extra level that is independent from the main space.

A mezzanine level effectively adds a new floor, or part of a new floor, to a double height space without necessarily creating two sections of equal height. It is a complex structural undertaking requiring careful planning and design. The size and scope of a mezzanine is dependent upon the overall dimensions and organization of your space. If extra space is essential to accommodate several individual requirements, such as an independent sleeping and bathing area for children, or a separate work area, consider inserting more than one mezzanine or adding mezzanines at different levels. Include independent access to each level, or galleries leading from one space to the next. However, even if it is possible to insert an mezzanine, it is counter-productive to do so if this will compromise a general sense of openness and light.

In comparison, adding a simple sleeping platform, large enough for a bed, reading light and alarm clock, is akin to fixing a top bunk. However, although very different in size and complexity, both options offer an opportunity to introduce a new structural and visual dimension to an open-plan environment. A new level provides two-way views, both out of and into the new area, liberates valuable space beneath, and offers a sense of separation without losing a vital connection with the main space.

Try to place a mezzanine or sleeping platform in a position where it will enjoy a special view of the interior, or has access to a window with attractive views. Bear in mind the importance of ventilation for basic health and comfort. If it is possible, perhaps insert a skylight above the new level to increase the flow of light and air, or position the new level where it will receive direct light from an existing window. Nothing can compete with the good effects of waking up to natural light.

opposite below and below
The imposing dimensions of a former period sitting room provide sufficient height for this space-saving solution. A compact sleeping platform fits above a kitchen area, and is accessed via a movable ladder. The platform overlooks the dining and sitting area beyond.

If space is at a premium, removing or moving a bed when not is use liberates·a considerable amount of space and adds flexibility. A dual-functioning zone, perhaps combining sleeping and working, or sleeping and a child's play area, allows you to put the space to good use during the day. Mobility, perhaps a worktable on wheels, or lightweight plastic storage boxes for toys, will facilitate the crossover. Assembling and dismantling anything on a day-to-day basis is over-complex and time-consuming.

Fold-up beds, where the bed lifts vertically into a storage box, are clever, convenient space-saving devices that facilitate flexible sleeping arrangements. They are ideal for a small space and also offer useful back-up accommodation. The key to fold-up efficiency is a lightweight mechanism for ease of use. Beware of labour-intensive manual designs – these are fine for occasional use, but will soon become a chore as an everyday option. One possible disadvantage of a fold-up system is finding adequate storage for duvets and pillows when the bed is out of the way. Perhaps build in a cupboard next to or above the folding bed box. Another flexible option is a bed on wheels that can swivel into place or out of the way according to the time of day or night. This will not clear the same amount of space as a fold-up bed, but it will shift the emphasis of a zone from one specific activity to make way for an alternative.

below In a sequence of simple movements, a fold-up bed swings vertically into a cupboard. Fixing shelves into the back of the recess provides extra storage for clothes and bedlinen.

left and above What first appears to be a cupboard in fact conceals a roomy double bed. When space is at a premium, a fold-up bed is an ingenious solution. The easy, gliding mechanism of a fold-up system requires minimum effort to operate, and it allows you to hide away your bed when not in use. Fold-ups are ideal for dual-functioning areas, as they free up valuable space for a different activity, allowing you to use an otherwise redundant area as a work zone or play area.

new york loft space

CASE STUDY 4 | LOW-KEY LOFT SPACE

In this light, white and functional New York loft space,

a textile designer combines a place to live and work

with ease and efficiency. Loose cotton covers on

armchairs, a long sociable dining table, energetic

dogs and sleeping cats and bundles of fresh flowers

project an overall sense of welcome, calm and

comfort. Yet this tranquil space is also the centre of

a buzzing international textile business.

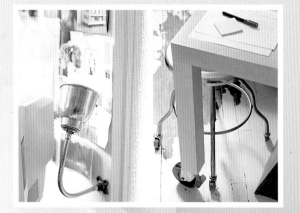

Formerly a sewing factory in New York's Tribeca district, this space is a low-tech conversion with exposed surface power conduits and low-maintenance scrub-down floors and work-tops. Four south-facing windows ranged along the length of one wall provide light for the whole space. The interior retains a sense of openness and light while providing different degrees of separation for living and working. It is a triumph of simplicity and invention.

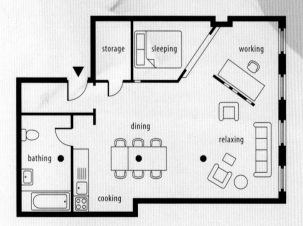

floor plan Access from a communal stairway leads directly into the main space. Three cast-iron pillars run down one side of the interior, with four south-facing windows along the end wall. An internal opening between the cooking and bathing zones allows natural light to penetrate the full length of the loft space.

The main living area, a logical sequence of everyday activities from kitchen to dining to sitting, extends the full length of the space down one side of the loft, following a line of decorative cast-iron supporting columns. Along the opposite side of the space is an imaginative arrangement of sleeping and work areas.

The sleeping area is a square box just large enough for a double bed, set one step up from the main space. Completely open on one side, with views across the living and work areas to the windows beyond, it benefits from a good source of natural light. A diagonal step running the full width of the opening adds an essential extra triangle of floor space at the bottom of the bed, providing a place to step into. Simple voile curtains pull across the opening to enclose the whole area behind a translucent screen. The change in floor level and the optional voile screen signal a different territory, a retreat from the buzzy world beyond.

The work zone projects a very different dynamic. A fixed floor-to-ceiling panel, studded with rectangular glass insets, is set diagonally across one corner of the space to create a semi-separate work area. The divider is

opposite inset left Functional without being overly industrial, clip-on task lights and pin boards define a low-tech workspace.

opposite inset right Furniture on castors can be moved around easily, promoting a sense of flexibility.

opposite below Aligning the work table behind a fixed diagonal divider effectively conceals office equipment.

this page Voile curtains and a change in floor level separate the sleeping area from the main space.

an ingenious architectural solution, allowing easy access on either side but also providing a degree of separation without interrupting the flow of space. It defines the compact work area yet at the same time promotes a sense of openness, light and connection.

Open shelving and a folding tray table provide low-tech but effective storage for office supplies and essential papers. A work table on castors is positioned directly behind the divider, providing a place for the owner's computer equipment and a base for general day-to-day activities. An inspiration board, fabric and colour swatches, beads, postcards and personal knick-knacks adorn the space, adding colour and detail. All in all, this is a compact, efficient work area, practically invisible from the living area opposite.

Developing the space is an on-going, do-it-yourself project, with the best ideas, like the sleeping platform and diagonal divider, evolving out of the owner's determination to fit all the requirements of a busy life into an imperfect space. The kitchen/dining table is another example of this approach – it splits into two separate pieces with a cut-out space in the middle to accommodate a cast-iron support column in the centre. How else to include a long table in an ideal position between the cooking and relaxing areas? But these clever details do not jump out or spoil the visual compatibility of the interior. The simplicity of a wrap-around white aesthetic, with white floors, ceiling, walls and fabrics, unifies any imperfections and quirky details and adds to an overall sense of space and light.

opposite The main living space is big, light and white, with a sequence of kitchen, eating and relaxing zones down one side. The work zone is set up behind a diagonal screen, which conceals it without separating it from the main space.

right Easy-access open shelving, base units and a tile splashback focus the main activity of the kitchen along one wall. The long table for food preparation, eating and working also provides a convenient drop zone for laden shopping bags.

WHETHER YOU DESIGNATE A SEPARATE AREA FOR WORK OR COMBINE ACTIVITIES IN

A MULTI-FUNCTIONAL ZONE, GOOD ORGANIZATION AND PLENTY OF FLEXIBILITY

WILL HAVE A BIG IMPACT ON YOUR EFFICIENCY AND ENJOYMENT.

working

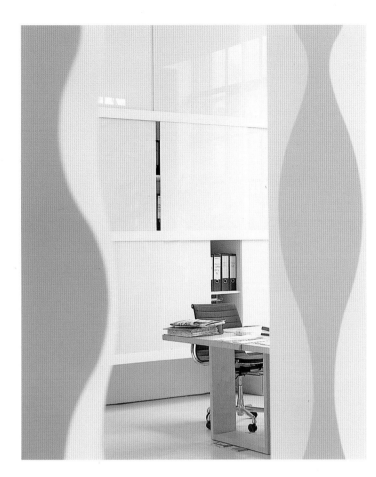

Investing time and effort in creating an enjoyable, comfortable and efficient working place is essential for health and well-being. If working and living in the same space is a permanent arrangement, then it is important to acknowledge this with a commitment to finding a place to work that enjoys a source of natural light and fresh air as well as a sense of space. This can be as simple as an area alongside a window that you can divide from other zones by a translucent screen, or as expansive as an entire mezzanine level for sole use as a home office. The big advantage of a permanent work space is that it allows you to leave everything where it is from one day to the next without having to tidy all your things away at the end of the day.

Setting up a work place in an awkward or badly lit area in an attempt to impinge as little as possible on your living space is a big mistake. This may seem like a good short-term option, but will soon

opposite A combination of hanging paper banners and a decorative folding screen effectively separate a work zone from a main living area.

left and above left Perspex panels set on runners screen shelves and slide along to give easy access to files, but conceal all when the space reverts to domestic use.

above Decorative items facilitate integration with the rest of your space and create a welcoming environment.

develop into an unhealthy long-term one. If you work from home, equipment, paperwork and space requirements are likely to increase, not decrease, so finding an area that can only just accommodate a working zone now is impractical as it makes no provision for future developments. You will quickly outgrow its limits and may end up hijacking space in other areas. It is far better to plan for the future.

If space is at a premium, then a dual-function area will offer you greater flexibility and freedom than an entirely separate work zone. A dual-function area does require a degree of transfer from one activity to another, but this can be as simple as wheeling a work table into the centre of a space. In theory, any area that is not in use during the working day is a possible option for a work zone. For example, if you can easily convert a light and open relaxing area into a place to work, this is a good option. If the conversion requires a minor compromise to an otherwise efficient arrangement, such as storing files in another area, then the benefits are greater than the inconvenience. However, if you require frequent access to the files then this level of compromise may be unworkable as an everyday arrangement.

Consider access to your work area. It is a good idea to choose somewhere our of the way of general household traffic and devise a degree of separation from the overall space. If you share a household with children who are at home during the day, taking over an area they like to use and denying them access will be problematic. If possible,

far left Reduce the visual impact and office-like effect of an extensive filing system by hiding files behind sliding panels, paper screens or even a simple roller blind.

centre left In a dual-function space, orientating the desk away from the bed to look out of the window provides a degree of separation.

left A desk tucked into a quiet corner may be all you need to pay bills and keep up with your correspondence.

opposite above and this page
In this inspiring conversion of
a former post office sorting
depot, half the space is
divided into two levels. The
remaining full-height space
is an artist's studio complete
with industrial-style lighting.

work somewhere less central or popular – it will create less conflict. Alternatively, invest in mobile furniture and storage and plan where to work on a day-to-day basis.

Good ergonomics play a key role in determining and designing an ideal work environment and are vital for health and well-being. If you spend several hours a day sitting down to type or draw, constantly repeating a sequence of similar movements, then it is essential to invest in a supportive, adjustable chair and an adequate table or drawing board. If you frequently refer to a filing system, easy access is vital. Depending on the type of

work you do, a kitchen table can provide a work area. However, the height of a domestic table is incompatible with an ergonomic position for typing, so this situation is not suitable for long-term keyboard use.

If you work on a computer, consider the position of the screen in relation to direct light. Avoid the glare of a back-lit screen or the mirror-effect caused by direct light on a screen. As light levels change during the day, modulate them with blinds. Supplementary task lighting is an essential back-up to natural light; it is not advisable to work long hours in an area without either.

opposite left In a compact New York apartment, an open-plan living and sleeping area undergoes a daily tranformation to a work zone for the two architect owners.

opposite right The space is full of clever details, such as a wall of floor-to-ceiling wooden panels that slide to one side to reveal flat-folding drawing boards.

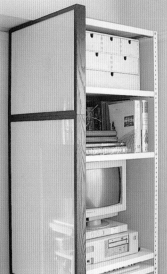

Setting up a work space in your home can require a big expenditure, especially if you need specialist equipment, so invest in flexible free-standing storage solutions and key items that can adapt to a review of your working habits or changes in circumstances. You can also take them with you when you move. Typical office-style furniture tends to look alien in an open-plan living space, so if you want to use this kind of furniture, it is best to screen it in some way. Traditional utilitarian metal filing cabinets and work tables look less unforgiving but lack the slick efficiency of new products. Check out creative and ergonomic alternatives in contemporary furniture showrooms or look in architectural or design magazines for details of suppliers.

If you do not need specialist storage systems, then use standard storage boxes and files. Avoid the children's playroom effect of colourful plastic bins and use metal, wood, cardboard or clear plastic containers. Low-level storage, such as boxes stacked beneath a worktable or a bench unit with lift-up lid, is less obtrusive than high-level shelving, wall units or cabinets. And custom-built furniture can maximize and individualize space.

above left The wooden panels open and overlap to reveal two drawing boards that fold up from the walls. The 1950s bar stools double up as office seating.

above Semi-translucent perspex panels set in a wooden frame hide high-tech office equipment and an industrial storage system from the main living area.

new york recycled

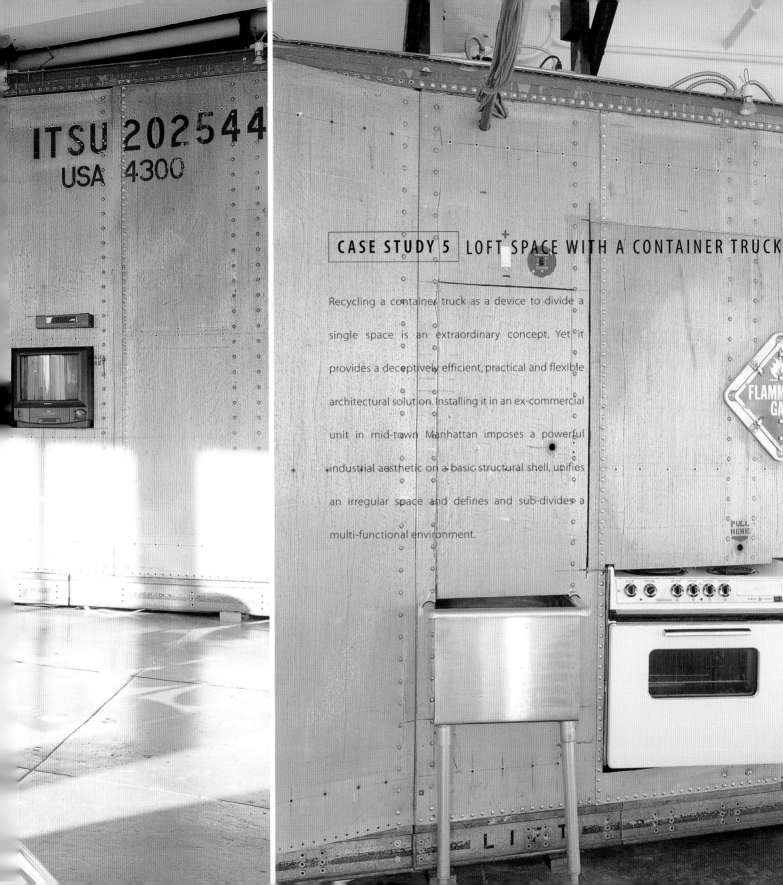

ITSU 202544
USA 4300

CASE STUDY 5 LOFT SPACE WITH A CONTAINER TRUCK

Recycling a container truck as a device to divide a single space is an extraordinary concept. Yet it provides a deceptively efficient, practical and flexible architectural solution. Installing it in an ex-commercial unit in mid-town Manhattan imposes a powerful industrial aesthetic on a basic structural shell, unifies an irregular space and defines and sub-divides a multi-functional environment.

FLAMMABLE GAS

PULL HERE

A photographer and theatrical set designer took on this ex-commercial unit with the intention of developing a versatile open-plan living and working environment. The challenge of a scheme like this, as with many open-plan multi-functional environments, is a complex question of how to organize space, prioritize and integrate activities and incorporate adequate provisions for separation. In this case, for a creative New York couple, a private sleeping area on view to visiting clients is unacceptable, whereas a big work-table hijacking much of the main living area is fine.

The space itself, a basic rectangle with an add-on square at the back, suggests a convenient and logical division into front-of-house and back-of-house activities. Also, positioning everyday appliances, like the shower, kitchen sink and cooker, along a single axis, simplifies division and separation. For the architects, establishing this single axis became the starting point for an inventive installation in keeping with their commitment

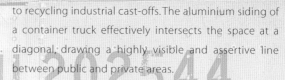

to recycling industrial cast-offs. The aluminium siding of a container truck effectively intersects the space at a diagonal, drawing a highly visible and assertive line between public and private areas.

The aluminium siding is cut into a number of different moving sections, all of which flip up, pivot or rotate to reveal different functions or areas within the space. The sections look rough and heavy, yet the mechanisms that control them are precise and efficient, so lifting and opening individual sections does not require any exertion. The ease of operation positively promotes flexibility and manipulation of space.

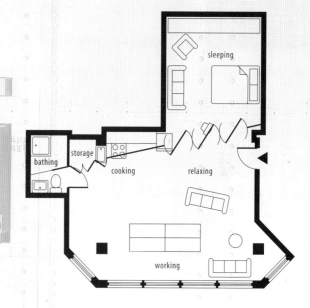

left Using the container-truck divider to house a television and video recorder underlines its involvement in the day-to-day activities of the loft.

main picture In the kitchen area, different sections of the truck siding flip up to reveal appliances, cooking and food preparation zones.

floor plan The space is an irregular rectangle and has windows along one side, next to the relaxing and working area. Two add-on squares conveniently provide a sleeping area at the back of the space and a bathing area off to one side. The aluminium siding of a container truck divides the space on a diagonal axis extending from beside the entrance straight through to the bathing zone.

A wooden frame props up the aluminium siding like a billboard and supports horizontal aluminium beams or rails running along the top and bottom of the siding. In the kitchen, two flip-up sections conceal the cooking and food preparation areas, with a cupboard door over the sink. Operating independently or together, the sections provide various combinations or degrees of openness. With all the sections shut, an abstract line-up

of appliances protrudes from the aluminium. However, thanks to frequent use, all or part of the kitchen usually remains open, providing vibrant background colour.

Separating the living and sleeping areas, three independent sections spin like swing doors, offering easy access and multiple variations of openness. Changing the position of the middle section also controls the angle of a built-in video and television. When the

section is closed, the television faces the main living area. When the section is fully open, it is possible to watch television from the bed.

The front-of-house area is a flexible living and working area, with the emphasis firmly on working. The central focus is one large workstation on wheels that contains everything relating to work. In theory the table can be moved, but in practice it is the centre of activity.

opposite The side of a container truck divides the loft diagonally into front-of-house working and relaxing areas and back-of-house sleeping and bathing zones. The kitchen area and appliances are part and parcel of the diagonal axis itself.

above left Recycling old commercial filing cabinets and lockers provides a wall of comprehensive storage.

above right When the panel containing the television swings open, the screen is visible from the bed.

one space
essentials

dividing | lighting | storing

ONE OF THE MAIN CONCERNS OF LIVING IN A SINGLE SPACE IS
FINDING WAYS TO SUBDIVIDE IT EFFECTIVELY. DIVIDERS ALLOW
YOU TO SEPARATE AREAS WITHOUT COMPROMISING THE OVERALL
SENSE OF SPACE AND LIGHT DISTRIBUTION.

dividing

There are many different kinds of dividers, but in general they fall into two groups. The first group consists of built-in dividers, which can be fixed, such as a glass-brick wall, or adjustable, such as sliding panels or sections of wall. The second group is made up of freestanding dividers, such as screens or large pieces of furniture. Choose dividers that will meet your individual requirements in terms of space, flexibility, overall aesthetics and cost-efficiency.

When assessing your individual requirements, think about the way you use your space. Do you need to subdivide the space daily, perhaps alternating between an open-plan relaxing zone and a separate work area, or will you want to subdivide your space more infrequently? Will you be happy with lightweight divisions between sleeping and bathing areas, or do you want to incorporate a more substantial partition? Do you require complete isolation in any part of your space – a child's sleeping area, for example? Using dividers to change the dynamics or mood of the space is another possibility, allowing you to transform an everyday space into an intimate one, or introduce a new configuration of space to suit a change in season or activity.

If you include permanent divisions as part of the fabric of your interior, they can compromise overall versatility, especially in more compact spaces. However, there are certain advantages to fixed dividers. A low-level partition wall sited between public and private areas, for instance, can incorporate the services and utilities for a kitchen or bathing area, or provide generous storage

opposite A simple wooden frame supports perspex panels set in a curve to divide living and sleeping areas and provide storage.

above left and centre Inexpensive curtain track hung with plastic sheeting separates a sleeping area from the main living zone.

above right Simple muslin drapes conceal a wall of storage in an open-plan living and bathing area and provide a degree of separation between different zones.

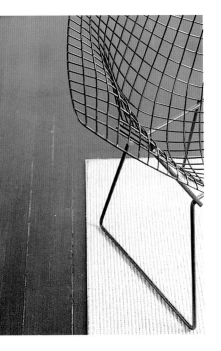

below A change in floor covering can act as an effective divider. Here, a change from wood to carpeting maps out different zones within a loft space.

space on both sides of the wall. To retain a sense of openness and space, create openings at each side of a fixed partition, or leave a gap between the top of the panel and the ceiling. If a floor-to-ceiling partition is essential for insulation or privacy, use opaque glass or glass bricks or knock through internal windows, which will boost light distribution and create a sense of connection throughout the space.

If you want fixed dividers as well as optimum flexibility, choose moving, sliding, swivelling, pivoting or folding panels. These will enable you to divide a space into several different areas without compromising valuable versatility or provision for privacy, allowing the interior to revert to maximum openness. Where a panel is stored when not in use and how easy it is to operate are both important considerations. When not extended, sliding panels usually cover a section of wall or overlap each other, or disappear into a recess in a wall. Pivoting or folding panels usually fold away flat in a recess in a wall, like giant shutters.

For sliding and folding panels, fit recessed metal tracks into the floor and ceiling to support the panels. If you suspend panels from a ceiling track, it is not strictly necessary to include recessed tracks in the floor, but doing so will add stability. For panels which disappear into a wall recess, fit retractable handles on the reveal.

Mobile screens can perform a similar function to built-in panels, but they give you the freedom to reconfigure space in any way at any time. Japanese paper and wood screens, folding or rolling wooden

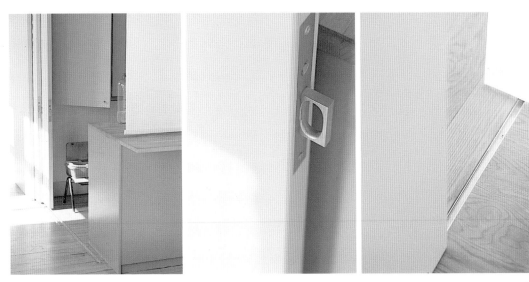

opposite left This kitchen area offers several levels of enclosure and division, with flip-down panels above work surfaces, sliding panels to screen it off and a roller blind.

opposite centre and right Panels with retractable handles on recessed runners allow for a frequent and efficient reconfiguration of space.

left In this New York loft, moving dividers facilitate easy and frequent changeovers from an open-plan gallery to two individual sleeping enclosures and a bathing area.

above A two-way opening opaque glass panel screens off a bathing area without blocking natural light .

screens and hospital-style fabric and metal screens all provide different degrees of separation and are appropriate to different styles of interior. Alternatively, make your own screens with MDF panels and flat hinges. Or, for a quick-fix solution, throw fabric over a free-standing mobile clothes rail. Large paintings, a sheet of perspex, fabric or paper banners, strings of beads or metal chains hanging from ceiling rails or hooks will all effectively demarcate space and will combat a lack of variation in a featureless interior.

Decoration and furnishings can also indicate a change in area or activity, effectively dividing a single space into several different zones. A change in floor covering, from concrete paving slabs to wooden floorboards, or rubber tiles to woollen carpet or rugs, can differentiate between a hard-working public area and a relaxing private one. Arrange furniture, especially key items like sofas and tables, in social groupings to define different activity areas. And use large pieces of furniture like book cases or cabinets to divide space. Colour can also unify or divide a space. Paint a wall or use a single-colour rug or a series of chairs in identical or co-ordinating colours to draw attention to a specific grouping or divide an open-plan scheme visually.

above left and centre A narrow bathing area between sleeping and working zones is separated from the living area with a sheet of clear glass. A sliding plastic panel fixed on the outside of the glass offers extra privacy.

above right and opposite This sophisticated track system supports corrugated-plastic panels that slide and overlap to divide private and public areas without blocking out light in a potentially dark semi-underground space.

LIGHT IS A VITAL ELEMENT IN ONE-SPACE INTERIORS.
IMAGINATIVE INSTALLATIONS CAN OPTIMIZE A SENSE
OF SPACE AND UNITY, PROVIDE A FOCUS FOR DIFFERENT
ZONES AND DEMARCATE OVERALL SPACE.

lighting

left and below In this former artist's studio, a sunny spot in front of a window provides a welcoming location for eating and relaxing. Venetian blinds control incoming light and can black out the space when darkness is required.

above A fine fabric screen on a sliding metal frame in tandem with roller blinds modulate the incoming light levels at expansive windows.

opposite In an ex-industrial space with large metal-frame windows, a banner of tracing paper hanging from a metal pole diffuses light, screens an inner city view and adds an element of privacy.

Looking at the way natural light affects different parts of a space is a good starting point for deciding how to organize an open-plan environment. It makes sense to devote the best-lit areas to key social zones, such as relaxing or cooking and eating. Any area with a good supply of light will always be a welcoming space.

If it is possible and cost-efficient to alter or reconfigure your space in any way, it is well worth increasing the amount of incoming light by inserting new windows or skylights or enlarging existing ones. Removing or reducing the size of internal walls, inserting internal windows or, in a space on more than one level, removing part of a floor to create a double-height opening, will all have a dramatic effect on light distribution and will enhance dark areas by providing access to natural light. White walls, ceilings or floors and glass walls or floors, especially on mezzanine levels or galleries, will all improve light levels and distribution. Shiny surfaces such as glass, metal and perspex will also animate a space by reflecting light.

Modulating the amount of incoming light is a relatively simple issue. Window treatments such as roller blinds, Venetian blinds or curtains all provide inexpensive solutions and offer privacy when needed. To diffuse incoming light and screen an unappealing view, hang paper or fabric banners or roller blinds at the window. If it is necessary to block out light completely, fit shutters or black-out blinds.

Use artifical light to supplement natural light and to add versatility and variation to a space. Artificial lighting falls into four groups: ambient, task, accent and information. Ambient lighting is general background lighting that throws light over a wide area. Task lighting illuminates one area to aid a specific task or activity. Accent lighting can highlight an architectural feature or decorative object. Information lighting helps you move around a space safely, illuminating a change in floor-level, for example. A combination of all four types will create a comfortable, flexible and user-friendly environment.

Different light sources and fittings create very different effects. Halogen lighting is cool and modern, while tungsten is warm and mellow. Fluorescent lighting can create similar effects to both halogen and tungsten, and has the added bonus of being ecologically friendly. There is an enormous range of different fittings available. The ones you choose will depend largely on personal preference, but it is important to make sure the fittings will do exactly what you want them to.

Central ceiling lights create a pool of light and can indicate a key area, such as a relaxing zone. Add other light fittings, such as floor and table lamps, to enliven the scheme. Spotlights throw a strong pool of light and can be adjusted to suit different uses and activities. Track and barewire lighting carry miniature spotlights, which can be individually angled, swivelled or adjusted, on tensioned cables. Uplighters and downlighters reflect

opposite left In a workshop conversion in Paris, a decorative central light adorns a simple eating area.

opposite centre A classic yet contemporary wall light in a modern open-plan apartment updates the original lighting scheme. The versatile aluminium fitting can be used as a spotlight or an uplighter.

opposite right Modern and minimalist in feel, track and barewire lighting offers a more flexible alternative to fixed spotlights.

below Adjustable chrome wall lights are used as uplighters and bounce light off a white ceiling to illuminate a reading area.

right Recycling a hospital light as a task light in this kitchen area is in keeping with the large scale of the space and the owner's heavy duty catering equipment.

this page A mix of fluorescent tube lighting concealed behind sliding plastic panels and a sculptural floor light animate and add colour to a pared-down interior.

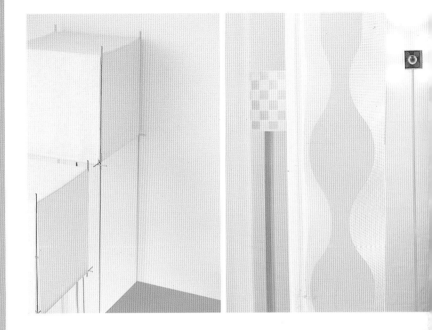

far right Decorative lights provide illumination but they also bring interest and atmosphere to an interior.

this page A simple detail like matching lights and paint shades transforms wall recesses into a focal point in a low-key relaxation zone.

light in a particular direction. Uplighters bounce light off the walls and ceiling and provide soft, diffused, overall illumination, while downlighters cast a pool of light downwards, like a spotlight. There are many types of uplighter on the market, in many different styles, while downlighters are usually discreet fittings, often recessed in the ceiling.

The arrangement and combination of different types of lighting can unify or divide a space just as effectively as any structural dividers by creating different effects, illuminating an overall space or focusing on a specific area or activity. In a multi-functional area such as a relaxing zone, fit ambient lights with dimmer switches and provide selective accent or decorative lighting for contrast. Use task lighting to signal areas set aside for specific activities such as reading. In a kitchen or a work area, it is essential to provide sufficient task lighting.

Installing new lighting systems can be disruptive, so wiring and attaching fittings, power points and switches should take place in conjunction with any other building work. Calculate how many electric sockets and light fittings you require for different activities or zones. In a space with a large floor area, fit sockets in the floor to provide maximum flexibility. A qualified electrician will be able to give you advice, assess your electrical infrastructure and let you know if your current system needs updating or extending.

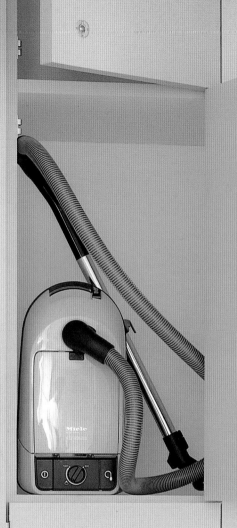

COMPREHENSIVE AND EFFICIENT STORAGE IS THE KEY
TO COMFORTABLE AND FLEXIBLE SINGLE-SPACE LIVING.
WITHOUT IT, EVERYDAY POSSESSIONS CAN DISRUPT A
VITAL SENSE OF ORDER, SPACE AND OPENNESS.

storing

opposite A large square capsule in the centre of a one-space interior contains bathing and sleeping areas as well as ample storage space.

right In a compact sleeping area, large-capacity drawers built into the bed base provide plenty of space for bulky items of clothing as well as spare bedlinen.

Providing adequate provision for storage is the key to organizing an open-plan environment. Storage solutions can resolve basic issues such as where to keep clothing and kitchen items or conceal bulky pieces of equipment such as televisions, washing machines and computers. In a multi-functional environment, good storage will help you to retain flexibility, visual simplicity and freedom of choice.

It is often more practical and productive to devote a substantial proportion of space to storage to ease pressure on a general living space, rather than maintain maximum space at the expense of comfort and practicality. In Japanese homes, where space is a critical issue, one-third of every household is taken up by storage. Although this seems like a disproportionate amount of storage to living space, sufficient storage can make a one-space home more flexible and versatile, allowing for simple and efficient changeovers between different activities, such as relaxing or working or sleeping.

Be realistic about storage requirements in a single-space interior. Creating a sense of space and order is not always about finding a home for every single possession, but about living with what is essential and functional. Edit your possessions and select a capsule collection of kitchenware, entertainment equipment, clothing and other key items, then design and plan your storage solutions accordingly.

above This low-level storage unit fixed to the wall offers a variety of open cubes, shelving and drawers. Units like this look unobtrusive and orderly and accommodate large amounts of essential equipment in a living area.

left Rows of identical cardboard boxes stacked in a basic industrial-style shelving system unifies and simplifies a collection of household items and clothing.

The basic options for different kinds of storage are either structural systems, such as a dividing wall with built-in shelves or cupboards, fixed systems, such as wall-mounted shelving or modular units, or freestanding storage items. All of these options can provide open storage for display or conceal items in some way.

The advantage of built-in storage is the freedom it gives you to use your space as effectively as possible. Many contemporary architects incorporate storage space in structural features, using perimeter or dividing walls to conceal streamlined floor-to-ceiling cupboards that can accommodate the essential clutter of everyday life. Built-in storage can also make use of irregular structural details or otherwise unused space in a way that ready-made storage items cannot, by tucking a custom-made clothes rail or drawer unit beneath a sloping ceiling, for example, or fitting drawers into stair treads. Fixed storage, such as wall-mounted modular systems, presents plenty of functional options for both concealed storage and display space. Freestanding and mobile storage is a highly flexible option, as it can be moved around from area to area as needed.

Different areas and activities require different storage provisions. In a kitchen area, the emphasis is on quick and easy access to key items. Store utensils that are in frequent use within an arm's length of the work area. Ideally, store pots and pans next to the oven or hob,

above left Sliding plastic panels conceal a wedge-shaped storage area, which extends the full length of a one-space apartment, from relaxing to cooking zones.

above right Suspending kitchen utensils from a stainless steel rail above a hob and oven means they are always within easy reach.

below left Open shelving fixed in front of a window is a focal point in a long, narrow kitchen area. The shelves provide storage space but do not block the light.

below right This precise, built-to-measure storage unit brings a splash of colour to a kitchen area and utilizes otherwise wasted space.

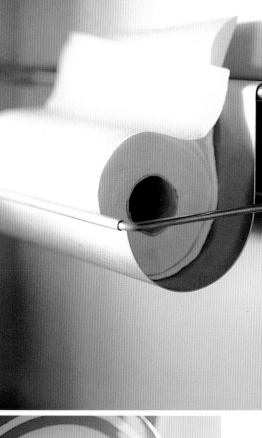

left In a compact space, clever details, like this sleek metal holder for a roll of kitchen paper, make the most of the available space. When not in use, this tiny food preparation area can be hidden away behind a pull-down stainless steel shutter.

below left Space-saving storage solutions, such as this hanging vertical plate rack, makes use of wall space and supplements plenty of open shelving and base units in a tiny urban kitchen.

below Laboratory-style units, a stainless steel splashback and glass shelving optimize the available space in this New York kitchen area with an industrial aesthetic.

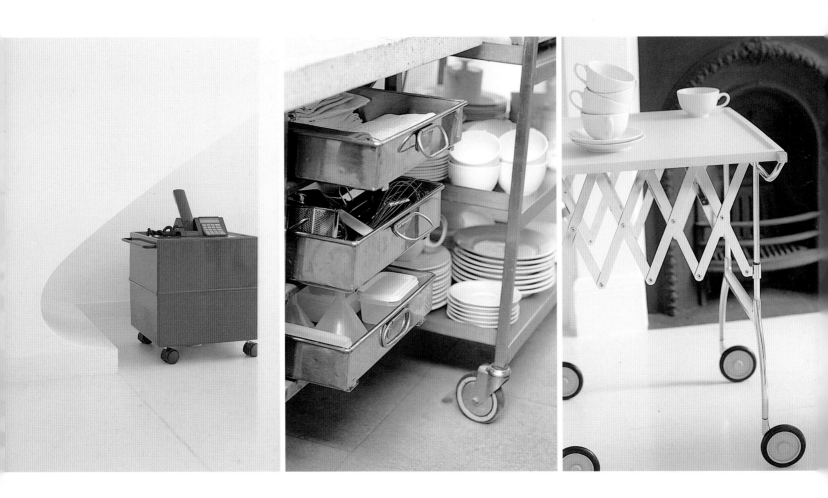

fresh vegetables adjacent to the food-preparation area and kitchenware in close proximity to the dishwasher, for easy unloading. When planning storage for a kitchen area, bear in mind that whatever you install is likely to be visible from the main living area, if not from every part of the space, so flexible dividers such as flip-up or sliding panels or roller blinds that pull down to screen the kitchen area will allow you to conceal clutter. Choose a combination of freestanding items and open shelving or fitted wall and base units, depending on your individual requirements and overall aesthetics. Low-level mobile storage units are space-efficient additions to any kitchen area and can be stored under work surfaces and wheeled out of the way when not in use.

Whether you spend time talking, watching television, listening to music or reading, a flexible storage system is essential in a multi-functioning living space, especially if you live as a family or with several other people. Leaving all your possessions in full view can look cluttered and untidy, yet if everything is hidden away an area can look sterile and anonymous. Aim to reveal a few items that represent different activities, but conceal large CD or book collections. Sliding panels, roller blinds or mobile screens can hide electrical equipment or a wall of books yet still allow easy access to items in frequent use. In a living area, storage options include wall-mounted units, low-level shelving or cabinets, freestanding cupboards or modular cube systems. A mobile computer desk or

entertainment system on a trolley is a flexible storage option, as it can be wheeled into a central position, then stashed away in a different area afterwards.

As well as storage items specifically made for the domestic market, there are many alternatives available from commercial or trade suppliers, such as catering, retail, office and medical storage systems. The large scale and utilitarian design of these products means that they fit in well with ex-industrial interiors. And on a practical level, items originally made to industrial or commercial standards provide greater storage capacity than their domestic equivalents. However, a filing cabinet or airline locker takes up lots of space, so avoid overwhelming a compact scheme with over-sized furniture.

opposite left A trolley with drawers acts as a mobile storage centre for CDs, videos, a telephone and directories

opposite centre Using second-hand catering equipment for storage is in keeping with the scale and industrial aesthetic of this kitchen area.

opposite right A versatile folding trolley stores away flat when not in use and provides an extra work surface in the kitchen area at a moment's notice.

above left This inventive custom-made storage system utilizes the wasted space beneath stair treads by using them as a chest of drawers.

above centre A metal bucket hanging from a rope and pulley can be lowered to give access to household items or raised so it is out of view.

above right Clever design maximizes the potential of this mini closet, with its fold-down ironing board and pull-out clothes rail.

a practical
approach

heating | insulation | ventilation |noise | assessing change

Creating an optimum living environment is a matter of individual choice, although fresh air and warmth are vital for everyone's well-being. And while simple joys like opening a window on a spring morning or lighting a stove in winter are rewarding emotional and physical pleasures, even the most elemental domestic space will benefit from some degree of automatic ventilation and heating.

In a single space, devising effective service systems requires precise planning and assessment. As a general guide, when choosing new service systems or upgrading, adapting or extending existing ones, consider all aspects of performance, cost of installation and level of disruption, running costs, aesthetics, flexibility and maintenance.

Many conventional domestic systems work well in open-plan apartments and conversions built to standard proportions. Yet the proportions and expansiveness of some conversions, especially former non-domestic spaces like schools, barns and light-industrial factories, often require a combination of high performance products and systems.

Heating In general, domestic heating is usually supplied via convenient, cost-effective central heating systems or by a series of independent heaters. Central heating systems are either wet or dry systems.

Wet systems heat water in a boiler using gas, electricity, solid fuel, wood or oil and distribute the hot water via pipes to radiators, convector radiators and underfloor heating pipes. Individual thermostats can set different temperatures on radiators and floor and wall convector radiators, whereas a single thermostat sets the temperature for all trench convector radiators and underfloor heating pipes. Wet systems usually heat the domestic hot water supply too.

Dry systems use gas, electricity or oil-fuelled heaters to warm air and distribute it through a system of ducts, grilles and convector heaters. A central thermostat controls air temperature throughout the system. However, with an additional cooling coil, dry systems can distribute cool air as well as hot, which is a big bonus in hot weather. Heating ducts transmit sound as well as air, so avoid placing machines or equipment next to vents or outlets. Both wet and dry heating systems take moisture out of the air so it is essential to keep fresh air circulating. Humidifiers and dehumidifiers can adjust air-moisture content. Alternatively, a simple bowl of water on the floor, Japanese-style, will restore moisture to dry air – drop in a pebble for visual interest.

Radiators, exclusive to wet systems, are available in every size, style and colour imaginable, and can be fixed to walls or stand on floors. They are usually made from steel, although cast iron and aluminium models are also available. Different configurations of coils and fins deliver different amounts of heat, so calculate performance in conjunction with aesthetics. Radiators are efficient, economical, easy to control and require little maintenance.

Bear in mind that in an expansive open-plan environment, with radiators attached to the perimeter walls only, heat can take time to radiate to the centre of the space. An electric ceiling fan, or series of fans, can aid the process. Alternatively, find a way of fixing a radiator, or radiators, in the centre of the space – perhaps using an existing architectural feature like a column. Incorporating an additional heating source, such as a stove or underfloor heating system, in the centre of the space will also prevent potential cold spots.

Good air circulation around each radiator ensures maximum heat radiation, so do not restrict air flow with big items of furniture like sofas or book cases. Depending on available wall space, this may present a problem. Radiators often occupy premium wall space, which can leave big pieces of furniture and paintings with no place to go. Work out

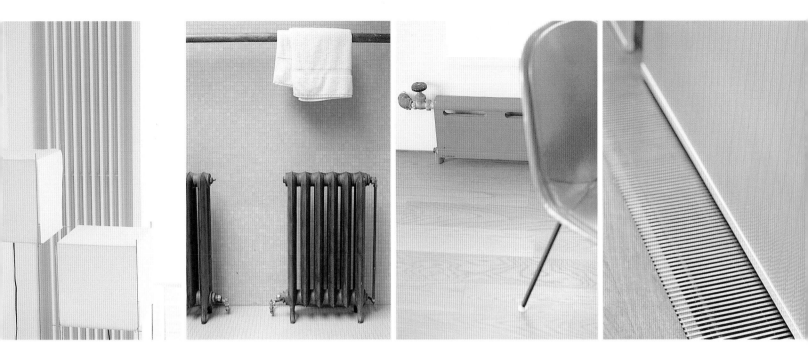

a floorplan before installation to avoid any conflicts. Finally, do not use radiators for drying wet clothes, as this will create a build-up of condensation.

Convector radiators blow hot or cold air and run on electricity or are connected to either wet or dry heating systems. Compact and unobtrusive, with grill fascias, they can be fixed to walls or ceilings or, ideally, fitted in trenches in flooring, beneath cabinets or in stair treads and skirting boards. For visual simplicity and to reduce the dust-trap effect of grill fascias, install convector radiators in a recess or box and conceal them with metal or wooden ventilation panels that are in keeping with the architectural style of the space.

Underfloor heating pipes, unlike convector heaters in trenches, will heat up an entire floor. This is invisible, high specification heating with a high comfort factor. Most underfloor heating pipes run off wet systems, circulating hot water through thermoplastic pipes set in concrete or an underfloor cavity. Installation involves pulling up the whole floor, so this option is a big

commitment, a big effort and a big expense. However, the water circulating through the system is not as hot as the water that circulates in a wet radiator system, so underfloor heating is cost-efficient to use. And if run in combination with a radiator system, it is possible to recycle some of the warm water. All-round good insulation is essential to minimize heat loss.

Stoves that run on gas, wood or solid fuel generate a great deal of heat and provide a striking focal point. They are capable of running a central heating system, but are most commonly used to heat hot water and boost central heating systems. Stoves are high maintenance, requiring regular cleaning and fresh fuel every few hours (except gas stoves), so are hard work on a day-to-day basis. Strict safety precautions apply for flue maintenance and installation, and it is advisable to check with your local authority about any fuel restrictions.

Other forms of heating worth considering include solar systems, which are eco-friendly, simple to install, require a good supply of sunshine, access to a roof to fit

opposite and above far left Vertical radiators are highly visible, so stick to simple colours and designs. Fitting them in a recess or niche makes them less obtrusive.

above left If you have the space, original cast-iron radiators provide substantial levels of heat. Sand-blast to remove paint and seal or oil to keep them free from rust.

above centre These basic, low-budget radiators are standard builders' merchant issue. They are low-key and unobtrusive.

above right A trench radiator with metal grille delivers heat all along a line of sliding plastic panels that separate living and sleeping areas.

solar panels or sheets and a back-up system for when sunshine is off the menu. Freestanding electric storage heaters provide low-cost background heating in a big space but they take up a lot of room. Electric fans, electric element heaters or gas storage-bottle heaters are all adequate sources of additional localized heat.

Insulation Generating heat is only one part of the equation – reducing heat loss and fuel consumption is just as important. Practical DIY insulating measures like attaching draught excluders to doors and windows, insulating roof space and lagging pipes, hot water tanks and storage cisterns will all significantly reduce heat loss. Professional measures like insulating cavity walls, floors and ceilings and double-glazing windows will maximize efficiency. However, it takes time to see a return on your investment in terms of savings on fuel bills. If you are planning a total refit of a space or major building work, incorporating these measures at the same time will be less disruptive and less expensive.

Ventilation Good ventilation is essential to prevent a build-up of moisture and condensation, which creates an unhealthy living environment and can damage the fabric of a building. Opening windows is the simplest way to keep fresh air circulating. Install ceiling fans in big spaces or areas away from open windows to ensure an air current. Fit ventilation fans to draw in fresh air and expel stale air. In compliance with standard public health and safety regulations, fit extractor fans in cooking and bathing areas – they will remove excessive moisture and potential condensation and eliminate smells to maintain a healthy, pleasant atmosphere.

Noise One knock-on effect of introducing heating and ventilation systems is an increase in noise levels. Incorporating good insulation in the fabric of the building will significantly reduce the amount of noise

entering from outside, and insulating pipes, boilers, cisterns and ducts, including at points of entry and exit, will significantly reduce internal noise.

Where possible, isolate and insulate domestic machines like tumble dryers and washing machines in a purpose-built utility cupboard or alcove. The rest is a combination, or possibly compromise, of planning and design decisions and individual aesthetics. For example, in simple architectural interiors with bare floors and walls, sound will echo and multiple in ratio to the number of people in the space. Using rugs to define different areas of activity and hanging fabric roller blinds will alleviate the echo problem and cut down noise transference. However, a degree of ambient noise and noise transference is a factor of one-space living.

Assessing change Reducing heat loss, fuel consumption and noise pollution and maintaining a clean and healthy living environment are all eco-friendly objectives. Deficient, out-dated services are inconvenient and uneconomical, so it is a logical step to replace them with up-to-date, efficient systems. Whatever level of change or installation you envisage, get professional advice to assess what already exists, what is possible and what products and systems are relevant to your requirements. Even simple projects like upgrading existing radiators on a wet system may require an upgrade in boiler as well. Likewise with electricity – it is essential to check electrical systems are safe and capable of supporting everyday requirements. New appliances may require new circuitry.

As a general rule, the simpler the layout of a system, the fewer the problems. Keep a plan of pipes, ducts and wiring to assist with maintenance and servicing. Quick access to stopcocks and circuit breakers is essential in an emergency – ideally install them in an area with easy access like a cupboard or behind a panel in the wall or floor and clearly label all pipes, switches and stopcocks in view.

this page In an expansive New York loft space, a row of double-height windows open independently to modulate fresh air and temperature levels and let in or keep out the sounds of the city.

stockists and suppliers

Help and advice

Architects Registration Board
73 Hallam Street
London W1N 6EE
0171 580 5861
The Architects Registration Board maintains a register of qualified architects.

The British Institute of Architectural Technologists
397 City Road
London EC1V 1NE
0171 278 2206
Architectural Technologists are concerned with the technical performance of buildings and can supply technical drawings and specify suitable materials for building projects. The institute publishes an annual directory of practices that have a BIAT member as a partner or director.

The Building Centre
26 Store Street
London WC1E 7BT
0171 692 4040
The Building Centre Bookshop stocks a wide range of useful publications covering architecture, surveying, engineering, building contractors, manufacturers, suppliers and trade associations. They also operate a mail order service that covers three main areas: Architecture and Design; Surveying, Planning and Development; and Building Services and Contracting.

The Building Centre Guideline
09065 161 136
This helpful telephone service provides general information and guidance on all aspects of building as well as product information. It can also provide information on different products, trade names and company names, as well as details of manufacturers.

Construction Resources
16 Great Guildford Street
London SE1
0171 450 2211
Britain's first ecological building centre, for advice and suppliers.

The Federation of Master Builders
14–15 Great James Street
London WC1N 3DP
0171 242 7583
Represents small and medium-sized building firms and issues a membership card to member tradespeople.

The Institution of Structural Engineers
11 Upper Belgrave Street
London SW1X 8BH
0171 235 4535
The Institution publishes a Yearbook of Members and a Directory of Firms for the UK and can put you in touch with a structural engineer in your area.

Royal Institute of British Architects Clients' Advisory Service
66 Portland Place
London W1N 4AD
0171 307 3700
The RIBA Clients' Advisory Service operates an extensive database on all RIBA registered practices and can put you in touch with an architect who practices in your area. Not all qualified architects register with the RIBA.

The Royal Institution of Chartered Surveyors
12 Great George Street
Parliament Square
London SW1P 3AD
0171 222 7000
The RICS regulates its members and will supply details of qualified members in your area.

Flooring

Dalsouple
01984 667233 for stockists
Rubber flooring tiles.

Gooding Aluminium
1 British Wharf
Landmann Way
London SE14 5RS
0181 692 2255
Sheet aluminium flooring.

Delabole Slate
Pengelly Road
Delabole
Cornwall PL33 9AZ
01840 212 242
Slate slabs for flooring, worksurfaces and fireplaces.

The Hardwood Flooring Co. Ltd
146–152 West End Lane
London NW6 1SD
0171 328 8481
Large selection of wood flooring.

Stone Age
19 Filmer Road
London SW6 7BU
0171 385 7954
Over 40 types of limestone and sandstone.

Kitchen manufacturers and equipment suppliers

Bulthaup
37 Wigmore Street
London W1H 9LD
0171 495 3663
Streamlined modern kitchens with good lighting and storage.

IKEA
2 Drury Way
North Circular Road
London NW10 0TH
0181 208 5600
Inexpensive modern flat-packed self-assembly kitchens.

Pages
121 Shaftesbury Avenue
London WC2H 8AD
0171 565 5959
An enormous range of professional catering equipment and accessories.

Stemmer & Sharp
Oblique Workshops
Stamford Works
Gillett Street
London N16 8JH
0171 503 2105
'One-unit' stainless steel kitchens in custom-built oak and glass cabinets.

John Strand
12/22 Herga Road
Wealdstone
Harrow
Middlesex HA3 5AS
0181 930 6006
A wide range of mini-kitchens.

Dividers

Armourcoat Limited
Morewood Close
London Road
Sevenoaks
Kent TN13 2HU
01732 460 668
Suppliers of unique polished hard plaster wall finishes that can be sealed and made waterproof.

Connections Interiors Ltd
Connections House
16 Stirling Avenue
Leigh on Sea
Essex SS9 3PP
01702 470 939
Mobile partitioning and screens.

Ergonom
Whittington House
19–30 Alfred House
London WC1E 7EA
0171 323 2325
Glazed and solid screens and moving partitions.

ICI
Telephone 01254 874000 for details and stockists
Manufacturers of a wide range of perspex, which can be used for mobile screens, partitions, doors, flooring and surfaces.

Luxcrete
Premier House
Disraeli Road
London NW10 7BT
0181 965 7292
Glass blocks in a range of different sizes and patterns, for commercial and domestic use.

Pella at WHN Distributors
1 The Quadrant
Howarth Road
Maidenhead
Berks SL6 1AP
01628 773 353
Top-hung sliding and folding doors, partitions and moveable walls.

Lighting

Atrium
Centrepoint
22–24 St Giles High Street
London WC2H 8LN
0171 379 7288
A selection of lighting and furniture from renowned contemporary designers.

*Babylon Design
Unit 7
New Inn Square
1 New Inn Street
London EC2A 3PY
0171 729 3321
Lights by up-and-coming designers.

John Cullen Lighting
585 Kings Road
London SW6 2EH
0171 371 5400
Made-to-measure lighting design for both house and garden.

London Lighting Company
135 Fulham Road
London SW3 2RT
0171 589 3612
*Wonderful selection of
contemporary lighting and lots of
advice and guidance.*

SKK
34 Lexington Street
London W1R 3HR
0171 434 4095
*Architectural lighting consultancy
and a stockist of cutting-edge
young lighting designers.*

Storage

The Holding Company
243–245 Kings Road
London SW3 5EL
0171 352 1600
*Comprehensive range of
predominantly small-scale
storage ideas.*

Muji
26 Great Marlborough Street
London W1V 1HB
0171 494 1197
*Large range of inexpensive but
stylish minimalist storage.*

Furniture

Aero
96 Westbourne Grove
London W2 5RT
0171 221 1950
*Manufacturer and retailer of a
sophisticated range of furniture,
lighting and storage systems.*

Century
68 Marylebone High Street
London W1M 3AQ
0171 487 5100
*Contemporary classic furniture,
specializes in 20th-century
American designs.*

Coexistence
288 Upper Street
London N1 2TZ
0171 354 8817
*A comprehensive collection of
contemporary European furniture.*

The Conran Shop
81 Fulham Road
London SW3 6RD
0171 589 7401
*One-stop shopping for
contemporary furniture, lighting
and accessories.*

Purves & Purves
80, 81 & 83 Tottenham Court Road
London W1 9HD
0171 580 8223
*Modern furniture, lighting and
accessories.*

Same
The Bridge
146 Brick Lane
London E1 6RU
0171 247 9992
Contemporary European furniture.

SCP
135–139 Curtain Road
London EC2A 3BX
0171 739 1869
*Contemporary European furniture
and lighting in one of the most
exciting showrooms in London.*

Space
214 Westbourne Grove
London W11 2RH
0171 229 6533
*Attitude contemporary furniture
and accessories.*

twentytwentyone
274 Upper Street
London N1 2UA
0171 288 1996
*Inspiring collection of mid-century
classics.*

Viaduct
1–10 Summer's Street
London EC1R 5BD
0171 278 8456
*Comprehensive selection of
European furniture and lighting in
an exciting showroom.*

Vitra
13 Grosvenor Street
London W1X 9FB
0171 408 1122
Contemporary furniture.

Architects and designers whose work has been featured in this book

Babylon Design Ltd
Lighting designers
Unit 7, New Inn Square
8/13 New Inn Street
London EC2A 3PY
0171 729 3321
Pages 14, 23, 100–101, 125 top right

Claire Bataille & Paul ibens
Vekestraat 13 Bus 14
2000 Antwerpen
Belgium
+32 3 213 86 20
*Pages 3, 18, 40–45, 121 left, 125
centre, 129 top left, 135 left*

Briffa Phillips
19-21 Holywell Hill
St Albans
Herts AL1 1EZ
01727 840 567
*Pages 26 top, 26-27, 62-63, 82, 83 top
left and below left , 128 top right*

Brookes Stacey Randall
New Hibernia House
Winchester Walk
London SE1 9AG
0171 403 0707
*Pages 1 right, 7 centre, 32-33, 68-69,
112-113, 116 below left and centre,
117 right, 127 top right*

De Metz Architects
Unit 4
250 Finchley Road
London NW3 6DN
0171 435 1144
*Pages 1 centre, 15 left and right,
92 all, 130 right*

Jamie Falla
MooArc
198 Blackstock Road
London N5 1EN
0171 354 1729
*Pages 25 below, 48 and 49 left,
66-67, 87 both*

Han Feng
Fashion designer
333 West 39 Street
12th floor

New York
NY 10018
001 212 695 9509
*Pages 17, 31 right, 50–51, 84–85,
88–89, 115 top right, 136 top left*

Fernlund and Logan Architects
414 Broadway
New York
NY 10013
001 212 925 4913
*Pages 7 right, 12–13, 46–47, 54–55,
83 below centre and below right,
116 right and 116–117 centre,
135 centre right, 137*

Alastair Hendy
Food writer, art director and
designer
Fax 0171 739 6040
*Pages 4, 10–11, 34 left, 72–79, 102
left, 120, 123 right, 124–125 centre,
130 centre, 131 left, 135 centre left,
136 below left, 144 centre*

Brian Johnson
Johnson Naylor
0207 490 8885
e.mail b.j.jon@btinternet.com
*Pages 2, 26 below, 56–61, 122 centre,
134*

Steven Learner Studio
138 West 25th Street
12th Floor
New York
NY 10001
001 212 741 8583
*Pages 52–53, 80–81, 116 top left,
123 left*

Littman Goddard Hogarth
12 Chelsea Wharf
15 Lots Road
London SW10 0QJ
0171 351 7871
*Pages 7 left, 70 top right, 71, 86 all,
92-93 centre & 93 right, 102 below
right, 126, 128 below left and below
right, 144 left*

LOT/EK Architecture
55 Little West 12th Street
New York
NY 10014
001 212 255 9326
Pages 28, 29 left, 106–111

Marino + Giolito
161 West 16th Street
New York
NY 10011
001 212 260 8142
Pages 104–105, 129 right

Orefelt Associates Ltd
Portobello Studios
5 Hayden's Place
London W11 1LY
0171 243 3181
*Pages 6, 24, 34 right, 102 top right,
103, 144 right*

Nico Rensch Architeam
0411 412 898
*Pages 25 top right, 35, 39 left, 64
right, 65 all, 121 centre and right,
122 right, 127 top left, 131 centre*

Evelyn Roussel
00 33 1 43 55 76 97
Pages 20–21, 118–119, 135 right

Stickland Coombe Architecture
258 Lavender Hill
London SW11 1LJ
0171 924 1699
*Endpapers, pages 8–9, 102 centre,
124, 128 top left, 130 left*

Totem Design Group
71 Franklin Street
New York
NY 10013
001 212 925 5506
Fax: 001 212 925 5082
*Pages 22, 114–115 main and top
left and centre*

Urban Salon Ltd
Unit D
Flat Iron Yard
Ayres Street
London SE1 1ES
0171 357 8800
*Pages 70 top left, below left and
below right, 129 left, 131 right*

Woolf Architects
39–51 Highgate Road
London NW5 1RT
0171 428 9500
*Pages 5, 19, 30, 30–31 centre, 64 top
left and below left, 90 below right,
91, 132–133*

picture credits

Endpapers Anthony Swanson's apartment in London designed by Stickland Coombe Architecture; **1 l** Gabriele Sanders' apartment in New York; **1 c** Nicki De Metz's flat in London designed by De Metz architects; **1 r** Nik Randall, Suzsi Corio and Louis' home in London designed by Brookes Stacey Randall; **2** Brian Johnson's apartment in London designed by Johnson Naylor; **3** an apartment in Knokke, Belgium designed by Claire Bataille and Paul ibens; **4** Alastair Hendy & John Clinch's apartment in London designed by Alastair Hendy; **5** Patricia Ijaz's house in London designed by Jonathan Woolf of Woolf Architects; **6** a house in London designed by Orefelt Associates, Design team Gunnar Orefelt and Knut Hovland; **7 l** an apartment in London designed by Littman Goddard Hogarth Architects; **7 c** Nik Randall, Suzsi Corio and Louis' home in London designed by Brookes Stacey Randall; **7 r** Jeff Priess and Rebecca Quaytman's apartment in New York designed by Fernlund and Logan Architects, painting by Rebecca Quaytman; **8–9** Anthony Swanson's apartment in London designed by Stickland Coombe Architecture; **10–11** Alastair Hendy & John Clinch's apartment in London designed by Alastair Hendy; **12–13** Jeff Priess and Rebecca Quaytman's apartment in New York designed by Fernlund and Logan Architects; **14** Babylon Design Studio in London Ltd.; **15** Nicki De Metz's flat in London designed by De Metz architects; **16 l** Christian Baquiast's apartment in Paris; **16 r** Nello Renault's loft in Paris; **17** Han Feng's apartment in New York designed by Han Feng; **18** an apartment in Knokke, Belgium designed by Claire Bataille and Paul ibens; **19** Patricia Ijaz's house in London designed by Jonathan Woolf; **20–21** Evelyne Rousell's apartment in Paris; **22** David Shearer and Gail Schultz's apartment in New York; **23** Babylon Design Ltd. studio in London; **24** a house in London designed by Orefelt Associates, Design team Gunnar Orefelt and Knut Hovland; **25 t** Andrew Noble's apartment in London designed by Nico Rensch Architeam; **25 b** Jamie Falla and Lynn Graham's house in London; **26 t** an apartment in Bath designed by Briffa Phillips Architects; **26 b** Brian Johnson's apartment in London designed by Johnson Naylor; **26–27** an apartment in Bath designed by Briffa Phillips Architects; **28 & 29 l** Jones Miller studio in New York designed by Giuseppe Lignano and Ada Tolla of LOT/EK Architecture; **29 r** Christian Baquiast's apartment in Paris; **30 l & 30–31 c** Patricia Ijaz's house in London designed by Jonathan Woolf; **31 r** Han Feng's apartment in New York designed by Han Feng; **32–33** Nik Randall, Suzsi Corio and Louis' home in London designed by Brookes Stacey Randall; **34 l** Alastair Hendy & John Clinch's apartment in London designed by Alastair Hendy; **34 r** a house in London designed by Orefelt Associates, Design team Gunnar Orefelt and Knut Hovland; **35** Andrew Noble's apartment in London designed by Nico Rensch Architeam; **36–37** Gabriele Sanders' apartment in New York; **38** Christian Baquiast's apartment in Paris; **39 l** Andrew Noble's apartment in London designed by Nico Rensch Architeam; **39 r** Christian Baquiast's apartment in Paris; **41–45** an apartment in Knokke, Belgium designed by Claire Bataille and Paul ibens; **46–47** Jeff Priess and Rebecca Quaytman's apartment in New York designed by Fernlund and Logan Architects; **48 & 49 l** Jamie Falla and Lynn Graham's house in London; **49 r** Nello Renault's loft in Paris; **50–51** Han Feng's apartment in New York designed by Han Feng; **52–53** the loft of Peggy and Steven Learner designed by Steven Learner Studio; **54–55** Jeff Priess and Rebecca Quaytman's apartment in New York designed by Fernlund and Logan Architects; **56–61** Brian Johnson's apartment in London designed by Johnson Naylor; **62–63** an apartment in Bath designed by Briffa Phillips Architects; **64 tl & bl** Patricia Ijaz's house in London designed by Jonathan Woolf of Woolf Architects; **64 r & 65** Andrew Noble's apartment in London designed by Nico Rensch Architeam; **66–67** Jamie Falla and Lynn Graham's house in London; **68–69** Nik Randall, Suzsi Corio and Louis' home in London designed by Brookes Stacey Randall; **70 tl & bl & tr** Lucy Guard's apartment in London designed by Urban Salon; **70 r & 71** an apartment in London designed by Littman Goddard Hogarth Architects; **72–79** Alastair Hendy & John Clinch's apartment in London designed by Alastair Hendy; **80–81** the loft of Peggy and Steven Learner designed by Steven Learner Studio; **82 & 83 tl & bl** an apartment in Bath designed by Briffa Phillips Architects; **83 cb & r** Jeff Priess and Rebecca Quaytman's apartment in New York designed by Fernlund and Logan Architects; **84–85** Han Feng's apartment in New York designed by Han Feng; **86** an apartment in London designed by Littman Goddard Hogarth Architects; **87** Jamie Falla and Lynn Graham's house in London; **88–89** Han Feng's apartment in New York designed by Han Feng; **90 tl & tr** Christian Baquiast's apartment in Paris; **90 br & 91** Patricia Ijaz's house in London designed by Jonathan Woolf of Woolf Architects; **92** Nicki De Metz's flat in London designed by De Metz architects; **92–93 c & 93 r** an apartment in London designed by Littman Goddard Hogarth Architects; **94–99** Gabriele Sanders' apartment in New York, **99** chairs from Totem; **100–101** Babylon Design Ltd. studio in London ; **102 l** Alastair Hendy & John Clinch's apartment in London designed by Alastair Hendy; **102 c** Anthony Swanson's apartment in London designed by Stickland Coombe Architecture; **102 r** an apartment in London designed by Littman Goddard Hogarth Architects; **102 tr & 103** a house in London designed by Orefelt Associates, Design team Gunnar Orefelt and Knut Hovland; **104–105** Chelsea Studio New York City, designed by Marino and Giolito; **106–111** Jones Miller studio in New York designed by Giuseppe Lignano and Ada Tolla of LOT/EK Architecture; **112–113** Nik Randall, Suzsi Corio and Louis' home in London designed by Brookes Stacey Randall; **114 & inset & 115 c** David Shearer and Gail Schultz's apartment in New York; **115 tr** Han Feng's apartment in New York designed by Han Feng; **116 tl** the loft of Peggy and Steven Learner designed Steven Learner Studio; **116 bl & c** Nik Randall, Suzsi Corio and Louis' home in London designed by Brookes Stacey Randall; **116 br & 116–117 c** Jeff Priess and Rebecca Quaytman's apartment in New York designed by Fernlund and Logan Architects; **117 r** Nik Randall, Suzsi Corio and Louis' home in London designed by Brookes Stacey Randall; **118–119** Evelyn Rousell's apartment in Paris; **120** Alastair Hendy & John Clinch's apartment in London designed by Alastair Hendy; **121 l** an apartment in Knokke, Belgium designed by Claire Bataille and Paul ibens; **121 c & r** Andrew Noble's apartment in London designed by Nico Rensch Architeam; **122 l** Nello Renault's loft in Paris; **122 c** Brian Johnson's apartment in London designed by Johnson Naylor; **122 r** Andrew Noble's apartment in London designed by Nico Rensch Architeam; **123 l** the loft of Peggy and Steven Learner designed by Steven Learner Studio; **123 r** Alastair Hendy & John Clinch's apartment in London designed by Alastair Hendy; **124 l** Anthony Swanson's apartment in London designed by Stickland Coombe Architecture; **124–125 c** Alastair Hendy & John Clinch's apartment in London designed by Alastair Hendy; **125 tl** an apartment in Knokke, Belgium designed by Claire Bataille and Paul ibens; **125 tr** Babylon Design Ltd. studio in London; **126** an apartment in London designed by Littman Goddard Hogarth Architects; **127 tl** Andrew Noble's apartment in London designed by Nico Rensch Architeam; **127 tr** Nik Randall, Suzsi Corio and Louis' home in London designed by Brookes Stacey Randall; **127 br** Christian Baquiast's apartment in Paris; **128 tl** Anthony Swanson's apartment in London designed by Stickland Coombe Architecture; **128 tr** an apartment in Bath designed by Briffa Phillips Architects; **128 bl & br** an apartment in London designed by Littman Goddard Hogarth Architects; **129 tl** an apartment in Knokke, Belgium designed by Claire Bataille and Paul ibens; **129 bl** Lucy Guard's apartment in London designed by Urban Salon; **129 r** Chelsea Studio New York City, designed by Marino and Giolito; **130 l** Anthony Swanson's apartment in London designed by Stickland Coombe Architecture; **130 c & 131 l** Alastair Hendy & John Clinch's apartment in London designed by Alastair Hendy; **130 r** Nicki De Metz's flat in London designed by De Metz architects; **131 c** Andrew Noble's apartment in London designed by Nico Rensch Architeam; **131 r** Lucy Guard's apartment in London designed by Urban Salon; **132–133** Patricia Ijaz's house in London designed by Jonathan Woolf of Woolf Architects; **134** Brian Johnson's apartment in London designed by Johnson Naylor; **135 l** an apartment in Knokke **135 cl** Alastair Hendy & John Clinch's apartment in London designed by Alastair Hendy; **135 cr** Jeff Priess and Rebecca Quaytman's apartment in New York designed by Fernlund and Logan Architects; **135 r** Evelyne Roussell's house in Paris; **136 tl** Han Feng's apartment in New York designed by Han Feng; **136 b** Alastair Hendy & John Clinch's apartment in London designed by Alastair Hendy; **137** Jeff Priess and Rebecca Quaytman's apartment in New York designed by Fernlund and Logan Architects; **140** Gabriele Sanders' apartment in New York; **144 l** an apartment in London designed by Littman Goddard Hogarth Architects; **144 c** Alastair Hendy & John Clinch's apartment in London designed by Alastair Hendy; **144 r** a house in London designed by Orefelt Associates, Design team Gunnar Orefelt and Knut Hovland.

index

acknowledgments

Thank you Andrew Wood for your great pictures and your appetite for photography, interiors, people, travel and sushi. Thank you everyone at Ryland Peters & Small for presenting me with this opportunity. Thank you Anne Ryland, Kate Brunt, Megan Smith and Annabel Morgan – in the order I first met you – for your commitment and interest in this project; your individual and professional input is evident in the book. Thank you Nadine Bazar for your essential contribution.

My biggest thanks to everyone living in a single space who said yes to photography and to all the architects and designers whose work is included. Thank you all for your hospitality, inspiration, imagination and originality. Thank you to everyone who gave me their valuable time and helpful information and suggestions.

Finally, thank you Lawrence Morton. And thank you Atom. Although I long to live in several places in this book, my home is the people I live with.